# KARNO'S DAUGHTER

# Praise for *Karno's Daughter*

'This is the most unobtrusive sort of great book: slim, fast-paced, chatty, peeling back new layers with minimum fuss or a throwaway sentence … *Karno's Daughter* manages to be uplifting and sad at the same time, a testament to the human spirit without being pedantic, tritely triumphal or showily sensitive.' —Jai Arjun Singh, *The Hindu*

'In a world where hardly one percent of the urban population has an idea of what constitutes our agrarian crisis, Rimli Sengupta chooses an interesting vehicle to impart information on how small-holding rice farmers in rural Bengal subsist … It's one of the best in narrative non-fiction that has been published in recent days in India.' —Suneetha Balakrishnan, *Kitaab*

'With an extraordinary empathy but without mawkish sentimentality, she transcribes Buttermilk's travails in a code that we understand. What she writes is interesting, how she writes, a pure delight!' —Sumitra Kannan, *The Book Review*

'Karno's Daughter is an easy book to read—the sentences are framed well, the chapters move quickly and there's no exaggeration of basic human suffering. It's a narrative that will leave you nodding your head in agreement and even, at times, tear you up.' —Smitha Verma, *Financial Express*

'Rimli Sengupta's writing is clear, fluid, and sympathetic … *Karno's Daughter* isn't a statement. It is a biography.' —Sonali Dabade, *The New Indian Express*

'Narrated alternately in the voices of the protagonist and the author, *Karno's Daughter* is a heartwarming and engaging story of a woman fighting for her basic rights.' —*The Times of India*, micro-review

'Sengupta's account of Buttermilk's world explains the complex routines that go into ensuring that her family has food even as she spends time preparing food for others.' —Vikram Doctor, *The Economic Times*

# KARNO'S DAUGHTER

*THE LIVES
OF AN INDIAN MAID*

# RIMLI
SENGUPTA

cntxt

First published in hardback by Context, an imprint of Westland Publications Private Limited, in 2018

First published in paperback by Context, an imprint of Westland Books, a division of Nasadiya Technologies Private Limited, in 2024

No. 269/2B, First Floor, 'Irai Arul', Vimalraj Street, Nethaji Nagar, Alapakkam Main Road, Maduravoyal, Chennai 600095

Westland, the Westland logo, Context and the Context logo are the trademarks of Nasadiya Technologies Private Limited, or its affiliates.

Copyright © Rimli Sengupta, 2018, 2024

ISBN: 9789360450052

10 9 8 7 6 5 4 3 2 1



Typeset in Adobe Devanagari by Jojy Philip

Printed at

*For M: she couldn't, so I had to.*

*The concrete gets tired of what it has to do,*
*It breaks and it buckles and the grass grows through.*

– Malvina Reynolds

# Contents

*'I'm writing about you, you know.'*

*'Write, go ahead, write.'*

*'You won't be able to read it, though.'*

*'I won't, but someone will.' A brief pause. 'God will, for sure.'*

# 1

# Crab

October in the Sunderbans in 1969 had a skin that looked like any other. The post-monsoon sky was a cleansed blue bowl. Below, the paddy fields heaved with grain. But all was not as it seemed. In that sea of green-gold was a red dot: a little girl, in a faded red frock, walking along a raised aisle. That's Buttermilk at six. She had a jumble of kindling on her head. Her arm holding it up could be another stick in the pile. She had foraged for hours to gather her load and was now carrying it home in the noon heat. Her empty stomach growled. Her mother had said she would eat once she completed this chore. She was hurrying home.

The crab was enormous. It was resting on ripe paddy, its blue-grey claws fearsome against the golden grain. Buttermilk saw it and stopped dead. This was not one of those palm-sized crabs common in the ponds and paddies around here. This one was clearly from the ocean, about three palms across. It basked in the sun, propped up on folded claws. She knew she had to catch it.

But how? Those pincers were scary. She set her load down and stripped off her frock. Naked now but for tattered panties, she crept stealthily towards the dozing crustacean. Nearing, she lunged, grabbed it by the claws with her frock as insurance, picked it up, and ran. It felt heavy. She ran, ran and didn't stop until she got home.

The day Buttermilk first told me this story she had been held up by weather. Slanting ropes of rain had lashed the city into a smoky whiteout. Her umbrella would've been worthless. She had to sit out the deluge before heading to her next job. Sometime before this I'd asked her what had brought her to the city. 'A crab!' she had said, her pudgy face creased with a grin. A crab? She had no time to elaborate that day. On this day, hobbled by weather, she did.

She has since retold bits of this story many times. Once, at the point where she strips off her frock, she bunched up her fingers into cones near her heavy bust and added playfully, 'I had little nubbins for boobs back then!' Another time, she was on her knees swabbing the floor under my desk. She stood up, her swabbing rag playing the frock, and mimed her lunge at the crab from nearly a half century ago. The claws folded only at a later retelling. 'How else would I grab them? They were fat,' she made a three-inch circle with her fingers, 'as wide as my arms were! It had folded them'—hands drawn in, chin on fingers—'and was quietly taking in the sun.' The story stays the same but she continues to add grain, like a fussy novelist.

When Buttermilk got home, her mother, Bashona, was in the kitchen. Buttermilk called out to her: 'Come out, Ma, right now! See what I've got!' She was breathless from running and the thrill. And also worried. She had disabled the crab's claws with her frock. But for how long? It was squirming. Bashona initially ignored her daughter's pleas and spat out a stream of cuss words. She thought Buttermilk was nagging her for food.

Food was not something Bashona could give her children that year. There was no rice to be had. The Bengal countryside had been ravaged the two previous years, first by a drought, then a flood. The year before that had seen a terrifying food crisis and riots on Calcutta's streets. There was rice in the fields this year but none in the larder. The government had flooded the market with cheap cornflour for a starving population. Buttermilk remembers the shock of going without rice for a whole year. 'It wasn't just us, everyone was eating cornflour. Ma would make a large vat of thin soup with it, sometimes with saccharin, sometimes with salt.' The memory brings on a smile, equal part odium and adventure.


Bashona had seven children. Often there wasn't even enough cornflour to go around. On those days, she gave the children chores. You ate only if you did your chore. Gathering kindling was Buttermilk's, which she was out doing when she ran into the crab. 'Ma thought I had brought back kindling and, chore done, was asking for food. So she stayed in and kept cussing. And I kept calling her.' A slip of a girl was raising a ruckus in a grassless courtyard with hutments around it, barely holding on to the writhing monster she had caught.

Eventually, Buttermilk's grandfather came out and chided Bashona: 'The child is panting and screaming in her underwear! Something must be bothering her. Can't you come out?'

Bashona reluctantly emerged: 'What is it?'

Buttermilk held out her prey swathed in her frock, 'Ma, look at this thing that I've caught!'

At this her grandfather rushed over. 'Good god, this speck of a girl has caught such a massive crab! Quick, here's a basin. Set it down, set it down!' And turning to Bashona: 'She's been calling you for ages. That crab could've lopped her arm off!'

Buttermilk was starving but bloated with pride.

Although the harvest was shaping up to be good that year, Buttermilk's father, Karno, didn't have a crop in the field. His family's land had been confiscated pending clearance of tax arrears. Back-to-back crop failures the two previous years had forced them to default. This year, Karno bought paddy in bulk from the grain market and brought it home. Bashona put in the patient labour of turning the paddy into rice: boil, dry, husk, de-chaff. Buttermilk remembers drifting off to sleep to the *thunk thunk* of the husking ram. Bashona worked into the night after finishing the household chores. Karno would then carry the husked rice to market. With the slim profits, he would buy cornflour for the family. The rice had to be moved in secrecy. 'That year there were a lot of police in the markets. If they caught you with rice, they took it all away.' Why? 'I don't know,' says Buttermilk, 'all I know is that both Ma and Baba worked long hours with rice and we still only ate cornflour.'

The Naxal movement was in full swing by late 1969. It had spread like wildfire through rural Bengal and spilled into other states. Indoctrinated students fanned out into the countryside with the mandate to recruit peasants into the movement. They attacked landlords and middlemen, sometimes killing them, and looted the rice they were hoarding in the face of surrounding starvation. The police ratcheted up their efforts to chase the Naxals down and disrupt their supply lines. Banning the movement of large volumes of rice would fit with this general goal.

Bashona shared her anguish with Karno: 'Our little girl has caught such a huge crab. There's no rice. How can I feed the children crab curry with corn flour?'

'Baba was always brimming with ideas,' says Buttermilk of Karno, her eyes shining with old love. 'He told Ma: why don't you make little balls with the flour? Then they'll have to chew on them. It'll be like pretend rice!' Bashona didn't like the idea. If her children were going to have a crab feast, it would have to be with real rice. She came up with her own scheme. From the two sacks of paddy she husked daily, she began to squirrel away a few handfuls of rice into a pan stashed under the bed. She needed time to collect enough. The kids hadn't eaten rice in a year, she knew they would devour mounds given the chance. Meanwhile, she kept the crab alive in the terracotta basin where Buttermilk had released it and checked on it obsessively.

A week went by. Karno got a whiff that something was wrong: the weights on his husked rice seemed slightly off for several days. One time when Bashona was out, he checked under the bed and discovered her stash. He confronted her that evening. 'Bawro-bou,' that's what he called her, 'Bawro-bou, listen to me, I know you're stealing the rice for the children. I know you're hurting because you can't feed them rice. You think I'm not? Tell you what, you give me that rice, I'll sell it and buy the broken damaged variety. We'll get twice as much. The kids will eat for two days instead of one. What do you say?' This made sense to Bashona.

Rice, once cooked, is rice. So what if the grains aren't whole? She had managed to stash away two kilos. The prospect of four kilos of broken rice made her happy.

Karno scraped up every last grain in the house and took it all to the market, along with the regular husked load. He was carrying nearly 150 kilos of rice that day on his cycle-van. Before leaving, he instructed Bashona that Buttermilk was to wait for him at the Khanrapara crossing. He would sell his load, buy the broken rice and hand it to her to carry home. So Buttermilk walked over two kilometres to the crossing and sat there waiting for him, flushed with excitement. 'Baba will bring the rice, I'll carry it home, and Ma will cook a feast with the crab that I caught!' No, walking back with four kilos on her head wouldn't bother her the least bit.

Karno had left home in the wee hours when it was still dark. He was being careful. But he ran into two policemen. They chased him. He pedalled away as fast as he could. When he thought he was far enough away, he dumped his entire load along with the cycle-van into a canal and hid in an adjoining banana grove. His focus was on hiding the sacks, he thought he could always retrieve them later and dry the grain. But the police had seen him dump his load. They came over to the spot on the canal, called in a few more hands, lifted the drenched sacks of rice and carried it all away. They also took the cycle-van.

After the police left, Karno weaved like a drunkard to the market and collapsed on the road, wracked with sobs. Buttermilk's eldest brother, Dada, had accompanied Karno that day to help out with the rice. He was ten. 'When Baba collapsed, Dada didn't know what to do. He had never seen Baba broken,' Buttermilk says, fighting tears, 'none of us had.' Dada ran home to fetch help.

Buttermilk's uncles rushed over and practically carried Karno home. Their house was in a churn, everyone in tears. The village had gathered.

Buttermilk, of course, knew none of this. She waited at the Khanrapara crossing. The sun became angrier by the hour. The impending meal of crab and rice took on mythic dimensions. The feel of the first mouthful was now a runnel in her brain, she had gone over it so many times. Rice, oh sweet rice, laced with the tangy heat of the curry, and the silk of crabmeat. Surely, as the hunter, she deserved a claw. Several hours passed. She sparred against the hunger and the heat but was wilting. 'Eventually Ma remembered. Dada ran over to fetch me. I kept asking him: where's Baba, where's the rice? He would only say: come along, Baba's home. I knew something was wrong. As we neared home, I could hear the wailing.'

Bashona did cook the crab that day, blinded by tears. She had to. She had seven hungry kids. Karno stopped squalling eventually and fell into a stupor.

'So, we didn't get to eat the crab with rice'—hot tears now—'we ate it with cornflour.' The sting, as if trapped in amber for decades, had lost none of its venom. Buttermilk was feeling it afresh, her face clenched and mottled with its effect. 'We kept the crab alive for eight days, but we still couldn't …' A sob heaves out of her.

Karno was penniless now. And he had no way to pay back the 150 kilos of rice he had lost. A distant uncle working in Calcutta said, 'What can you possibly do in the village now, Karno? You have to save the children from starving. Come to Calcutta.' He helped set Karno up and found him a room in the slum where he lived, at Ponchanontola. Karno initially came alone. The family joined him a few months later in the middle of 1970.

'That's how I came to the city. I was seven.' Buttermilk wiped her face with the end of her limp sari. Outside, the rain had let up.

2

# Work

Buttermilk is running late today. She's woken at 4.30 a.m. instead of the usual 4 a.m. Must be the indigestion that kept her up for a bit last night. She rushes through her morning routine in the pre-dawn quiet. Her home is spotless: two compact rooms opening onto a covered porch. One room she shares with her husband, who is away at the village now for the upcoming harvest. In the other, her son and daughter-in-law are fat with sleep. A corner of the porch is her kitchen. She makes tea and slurps it faster than usual. Her toilet and bath are out in the small yard, next to the veggie patch. While bathing she decides laundry will have to wait until the evening. She soaks the three saris she used yesterday in a bucket. Her bedtime sari that she wears after her post-work bath is thin printed cotton, soft and airy. For work, a synthetic sari is best because you can stretch better—all those hard-to-reach places when swabbing the floor on your knees. But synthetic is too warm for the commute. You're always packed like sardines on the trains. And then the walk from shift to shift in the hot sun. A sturdy cotton weave then, like a dhanekhali. If she can manage two of each type, new or used, her sari needs are sorted for the year.

It's nearly 5 a.m. Breakfast will be on the go. She stuffs two handfuls of puffed rice into a paper bag and heads out. As she walks, an April day breaks over Subhashgram, a deep southern suburb of Calcutta. In winter, this hour is a sticky dark; in the rains, it's the mud that's sticky. Buttermilk's routine is the same all year. She walks at a fast clip, a brawny woman on the thick side of average, past squat brick-and-mortar homes, most with no plaster or paint, more lovely inside than out. She watches out for rocks and sudden dips. This part of the road is gravel and dirt, the street lights few and far between. She's decided to take a shortcut. There's time before her 5.40 a.m. train, but she has sensed a bout of the runs coming on. The paved road offers less privacy. Luckily, the light is still murky and there's no one around. Buttermilk finds a corner and squats. A couple of curious dogs come barking. 'Shush, you,' hisses Buttermilk, 'there, go find Bonomali. Bonomali. Can you find him?' The name acts like a charm. Tails wagging, the dogs scamper off in search of Bonomali: Buttermilk's son, lover of stray dogs and street drugs.

Buttermilk always carries a bottle of water for such emergencies. She scavenges empties off the streets. It is better this way. Public toilets cost money and the local trains have none. By the time she arrives at Subhashgram station it's 5.30 a.m. The usual gang has already gathered: Aaroti, Shondhya, Shokuntala, Pawddo and a dozen others. These are women Buttermilk knows. The platform is teeming with a hundred others. All shift-work maids, waiting to catch the 5.40 a.m. into the city. They snatch a bit of chinwag before the train trundles in. Buttermilk and her friends have commuted together every day for over twenty years. But their pictures of each other are sketchy, as if downloading on a slow connection. There's never enough time.

To an ordinary eye, the train is already brimming, yet a hundred more get on. This is how it works. Each train car has an aisle, and on either side there are pairs of seats facing each other, each designed to seat three. During rush hours, those three-seaters seat four. And in between the knees of the lucky eight, stand eight more women: four facing one set of sitters, four the other, their buttocks touching. And the aisle, of course, is full as well. On the train today, a seated woman, evidently unable to bear the tectonic pressure, raises a mild whine when a seventh woman slides in past her knees. The rebuke is instant and collective. 'You sound like you're a newbie!' 'Why don't you stand and let her sit instead?' 'There's going to be another person going in past your knees, y'now.' There are rules here, for letting people in and out through a solid mass of humanity, at train stops that last barely a minute. Knowing them is paramount. Because one injury is all that stands between you and ruin.

Buttermilk reports at her first home in Tollygunge by 7 a.m., on kitchen duty. 'This elderly couple eats several vegetable dishes daily. It's a ton of prepping. A shaak green picked through and chopped. Pointed gourds, tips off and quartered. Then, let's say, a bottle gourd diced. I cook lunch. And then madam might say she'll make a stir-fry for dinner herself, and wants me to prep that: slice onions, chop green beans, shred cabbage. Not in large volumes mind you, just for two.'

A piece-work maid like Buttermilk is paid by the tasks performed. Cooking, the best-paying piece, requires skill but consumes time. A kitchen shift might combine cooking with dishwashing, charged as a separate piece. A cleaning shift comprises one or more of these three pieces: sweep and swab floors, hand-wash and hang up laundry, dust furniture. Cleaning work is hefty, demanding brawn. Cooking, albeit relatively light, comes with its nicks and blisters. Buttermilk does both types of shifts. Her hands are a scrapbook of scars. Her knees have fleshy black calluses from decades of swabbing floors on them. Her fingertips are worn to the point where her fingerprints look patchy. This presents a problem since she can't sign her name either; someone taught her how, but she doesn't have time to practise. 'It comes out different every time!' she complains.

Buttermilk's five other homes are in a tight cluster in Ballygunge, about two miles away from Tollygunge. She covers the distance on foot to save the bus fare. En route she cuts through the spacious park at the Dhakuria Lakes, a favourite with the morning walkers of south Calcutta. 'My daughters often tell me to quit the Tollygunge home. Too much walking, they say. I tell them, think of it this way: if the babus can go on their morning walks, so can I!' says Buttermilk with a belly laugh, and then adds, 'But honestly, I like the walk. I enjoy the breeze through the trees, the water. And it reminds me of my childhood.'

The Dhakuria Lakes are a short hop from the Ponchanontola slum where Buttermilk grew up. The place is sticky with memories. This is where she reached the magic age when the world unfurls around you. But Karno strictly forbade his children from hanging out at the Lakes. A walk through it is freeing, a reminder of the benefits of age.

She arrives at her third house by 9.30 a.m. When I answer the doorbell, she's usually sitting on the landing, eating her bag of puffed rice.

Buttermilk has been my maid for eight years. She comes in daily for an hour to clean the floors and do the laundry. When I'm away, she lets herself in at the usual time and also keeps my terrace garden watered. One time, having fled a particularly blistering May in the city, I returned to gleaming floors and the garden aglow. She dismissed my frothy relief with a mock attack: 'What did you expect me to do during your slot, roam the streets and get baked to pumice?'

Simply put, Buttermilk makes my life possible. For this, I pay her a monthly salary that just about covers dinner for two at a nice restaurant. She gets an annual raise, a month's bonus at Durga Puja, and a flexible leave plan that she prefers over a fixed day off per week. If she needs a few months' salary in advance, which is not infrequent, I provide it. Every urban home in India has a Buttermilk. Their work is unprotected by labour laws or unions. If they ever got together—an estimated eight million—and went on strike, the economy would grind to a halt. But they won't. Where's the time?

I'm certain that Buttermilk finds me inscrutable. She once scolded me for not having had children: what kind of outlandish life was that? I could tell that she'd been holding it in for months before letting out this plume of maternal energy. She's only a couple of years older than me, but she's a grandmother. She worries for me. Because my laundry suggests that I don't really leave the house with any degree of regularity, she suspects I'm unemployed. All she sees me do is sit at my desk staring at a screen, rarely unhappy to be distracted by her chatter.

Buttermilk is my portal to India's motile core. It seems to me that she and her ilk are leading lives of maximal vigour—hard lives, brutal even, but rich with community and a vast knowledge span, ranging from the recycle value of a dead laptop to the special knot that keeps a threshed rice bundle from falling apart. My urban life is anaemic in comparison, as are the lives of her purely rural compatriots. Like the Vamana avatar, Buttermilk straddles all three realms—the village, the suburbs, the city. She lives in the middle, with easy access to the other two.

Buttermilk waits at Ballygunge station for the 2 p.m. train back. She has done her six homes: cooked in some, cleaned others, their floors ranging from Italian marble (Marwari) to classy mosaic (Bengali old money). She has harvested discarded window grilles from one of those homes and is carrying them to Subhashgram for future use. They'll be perfect on her covered porch. She's always ferrying the city's refuse on the train home to feather her nest: discarded furniture; ash from the coal braziers of ironing vendors, excellent for fertilising her veggie patch; even rubble from construction sites. Like a potter wasp bearing bits of mud, Buttermilk has carried bags of rubble over countless trips to raise the foundation of her home. It no longer floods in the rains.

She's on the train and mentally winding down for the day when her phone rings. It's her husband: her mother-in-law is ill, Buttermilk will need to go to the village to help out. She calls her son to come to Subhashgram station to pick up the grilles. The same train continues an hour further south to her village. She gets there at 3.30 p.m. After a very late lunch and a brief rest, she freshens up the mud floor with cow dung, and then cooks dinner. Her mother-in-law is not up to these tasks today. By the time she gets back home to Subhashgram, it's 9.30 p.m.

But it's been a good day. There were no mishaps. The sole of her slipper didn't open up in a maw and make her trip while crossing the tracks. Her wallet, which she keeps tucked inside her blouse, didn't get picked in the train's melee. Above all, her daughter-in-law seems to be in fair weather and has dinner ready. Buttermilk's guts are in a churn from eating at the wrong times, but she sits with her family for dinner. There's time for a little TV before exhaustion takes over. Five hours of sleep is all she needs to be as good as new the next day.

Some days are not this good.

She came late to work one day, after a no-show the day before. I had lined up a few words for her but they skittered away when I noticed her bruised arm. Her eyes were dull with pain. She was limping. What happened?

It was that part of the monsoons when every bit of stationary leather grows a patina of mould. And public transport inevitably lists under the rain. In the crush when boarding the train to work the day before, she'd inadvertently hit a woman with her umbrella, who then yanked it out of her hands and shoved her. Buttermilk tumbled backwards just as the train began to pull away. She fell onto the platform, her purse landing a little distance away. Her cellphone was shattered. She lay there winded and hurt for a while before she could get up and go see a doctor. This is why she'd missed work yesterday. The train carried away the perpetrator, who kept the umbrella.

The following day, Buttermilk came to work with the story of what had transpired on the moving train that left without her. It was full of her friends on their commute into the city. They accosted the perpetrator, a young woman, and roundly berated her: 'If you were hurt, you could've argued with her *after* helping her onto the train, that's what we do in this line of work! How could you push her off the train?' They forced her to say where she lived, took her off the train and dragged her home—essentially under arrest. Her husband was livid, beat her up and took her to Subhashgram station. By then Buttermilk had collected herself and left. The husband found out which train Buttermilk takes on her way home from work. The next day was the day she came to work bruised and in pain. At the end of her workday, she got off the train and found the man sitting at the station, with his wife and several of Buttermilk's friends who had witnessed the incident. The young perpetrator had a bruised face. The man came up to Buttermilk and said, 'Aunty, she made a mistake, I've really beaten her up. Please forgive her this once.' His wife could barely speak but said sorry. The man handed Buttermilk her umbrella back and 200 rupees. She accepted the apology. All parties walked away satisfied.

I was struck by how her community had rallied to forge swift justice, however crude. Buttermilk brushed it off. 'This is a given. Who has the time to mess with the police? You know how the saying goes: a brush with the tiger gets you eighteen sores. Not to mention the bribes.' Her main takeaway was that her injury was minor. And that was chalked up to fate, like everything else that happens, good and bad.


My relationship with Buttermilk is largely one-sided. She seems glad that I bear witness; sometimes she's glad to simply unburden herself. Neither of us tries to scale the barriers to reciprocal sharing. On the rare occasion that we do have an object of overlap, our relationships to it are vastly different. For instance, hanging folders.

I recently got around to clearing out a large stash of research notes after clinging to them for a decade. This generated a small mountain of paper and dozens of hanging folders. Our paper and electronic waste belongs to Buttermilk, who usually takes it to the corner scrap dealer for cash. I was expecting the same this time. But why was she fishing out the folders and setting them aside? 'Do you have any idea how much fuel I need? I scramble daily for wood. Remember that cyclone a few years ago when trees fell all over the city? I had lugged two logs back to Subhashgram. Guess how much rice I cook every day—three kilos! Dal–torkari on top of that. My husband and son are both big eaters. If I use gas to cook rice, I'd burn through a cylinder every two weeks.' She caressed the sturdy American folders and pronounced, 'These will burn well.' The cremation of my folders would help feed two hearty rice eaters.

These two hearty eaters are Buttermilk's heaviest crosses. Tall strapping men with strong hands but 'empty upstairs', she says, tapping at her temple.

3

# Stormy

Three men walk towards Bermal, a village in the Sunderbans. There is an air of ceremony in their outfits: white kurta of fine cotton worn atop white dhuti with a striped border. Karno is in the lead, a small man, wiry and taut. Behind him are his brother Kaka and father Thakurda, taller but limp. The men are taking the long route from the train station, cutting through the rice paddies in the outskirts of the village. When it comes to finding a potential match for your daughter, it is best to see things for yourself. It's late April and the winter rice is amidst harvest. The fields are a hive of activity. The moist heat feels like it might be enough to curdle an egg. The three men walk, their fine shirts wet now and clinging to their backs. They are looking for someone. Kaka is the first to spot him, 'There he is, that's Jhoro.' A pitch-dark youth, tall and well built, is hoeing out the straw stubble from a freshly shorn patch. His back is to the visitors. A thin cotton towel is wrapped around his head to stop the sweat from blurring his vision. The men pause on the raised aisle at the edge of the field and watch the mid-morning sun ripple off the boy's muscles. Karno turns to the other two, his eyes alight with a triumphant smile.

Two days before, the boy's family had similarly eyed his daughter. Buttermilk had just turned eighteen: a shapely girl, spirited and hardy, with an almost pretty face. Word had gotten around. As her daughters reached puberty, Bashona wanted them out of the Ponchanontola slum; the living situation was far too brittle. Her solution was to place them as live-in maids, protection and income at one stroke, and guaranteed food besides. Buttermilk had been working as a live-in help at a Ballygunge home for over five years when her match came calling. She was happy in her work, but of course no one had asked her. The groom's family came to see her in the slum. 'I had to take half a day off work. Ma had cooked a meal for them. My job was to serve it. That's how they show you off, you see. Your shape, your gait, your manner. I don't know what they saw, I didn't look up. But I could hear that they were pleased. Very pleased.' And unusually, the family demanded no dowry. As a man with four daughters to marry, this was a big break for Karno. So much so that he didn't stop to find out why. He rushed headlong into the match.

After watching the groom work the field, when the three men eventually arrived at his family homestead, they were even more impressed. They saw four silos of rice being filled with fresh grain from the harvest. That spelt a lot of land. The house itself was two-storeyed, its frame made of saal wood. Karno couldn't believe it. Could his daughter really be this lucky? A hardworking boy, all this land, a two-storeyed house! He was going to be able to marry her back into the village, back into land. Land that he'd been forced out of. The three men consulted briefly and gave their word. The match was a done deal.

On their walk back to the station, they paused next to a canal for a smoke. A clutch of cowherds were hanging out nearby, shooting the breeze while looking out for the grazing cattle. The three visitors overheard their conversation.

'Have you heard? That Haldar boy is getting married again!'

'Which Haldar boy? The one in Bermal? Awrowali's son-in-law?'

'Yeah, the son-in-law!'

'Who, Jhoro?'

'Yeah, yeah, Jhoro's doing it again!'

Karno asked Kaka, 'Did you hear that?'

Kaka replied, 'I was just going to ask you the same thing.'

'I heard it too,' said Thakurda.

'So we've all heard it,' Karno said. 'You two wait here and finish your smoke, I'm going to go talk to those boys.'

His body language got the boys nervous. One of them yelped, 'What do you want?' as they wriggled away. Karno convinced them that he was harmless and when they eventually came closer he asked: 'What was it that you guys were saying? Who's marrying?'

They said: 'It's Awrowali's son-in-law.'

Karno said: 'Son-in-law? What's his name?'

'Jhoro.'

Karno tried to keep a lid on his shock. 'Jhoro was married before?'

'Yeah, didn't you know? He was married. His wife left him.'

'Where did she go?'

'To Chapla, back to her father's.'

'Is she still there now?'

'Yup, as far as we know.'

Karno came back to the two waiting men and slumped to the

ground: 'I'm ruined!' So this is why they were willing to take his daughter without a dowry. Thakurda, more cautious than his son, said, 'Wait, we have to get better information.' They had given their word and their word was gold. They had to make it work somehow. The groom's family were in-laws now. Even though they had withheld crucial information, their honour had to be protected. The men made discreet enquiries so that the in-laws suffered no loss of face. This is what they chose to keep from what they found: Jhoro was a good boy, hardworking if a bit of a simpleton, and the first wife had walked out because she had problems. Thakurda, the patriarch, made the call: 'Since I've given my word, let's go ahead with this. We three are the only ones who know. Our lips are sealed until the wedding festivities are over.' Not only did they not breathe a word to Buttermilk, the men also kept the news from their wives. The wedding went ahead and Buttermilk became a married woman.

That the groom had been married before was not the most serious tragedy. Karno, in his rush, had overlooked a strong clue in the groom's name: jhoro is Bengali for stormy. If Jhoro ever went to a psychiatrist—to a villager, a laughable proposition —he would likely be diagnosed with congenital dementia. His mental impairment hobbled him as a provider. Moreover, it ran in the male line of the family. His father had been afflicted, and so might his future son. This is likely why his first wife had left. Unbeknownst to Buttermilk, her elders had just put her on the path of a storm that would spawn many more, some raging as others ebbed, throughout her life.

The men came clean with the women only on the fifth day after the wedding, when the bride returns to her parental home for the turmeric-removal ceremony.

A livid Bashona withdrew into her kitchen and let loose a torrent of bile at Karno. 'Eh, was this girl such a burden? She was working so well. What was the rush? You threw the first one straight into fire. It's only been a year and you do the same with the second one?'

Karno had combed high and low to marry off Buttermilk's elder sister Didi just the year before and that match was a disaster.

The men tried to pacify their wives: 'We heard the full story only after we had already given our word. What could we have done? We had to proceed. At any rate, we've made enquiries. This is a good boy. It'll all work out.' The deed was done.

And what of the fresh bride? Buttermilk gets goosebumps as she recalls that morning. 'I wept alone on the porch, repeatedly grilling god: thakur, why did you crack my forehead this way? Then I heard Thakurda call me. "Dhupi re"—he used to call me Dhupi—"Dhupi, sweetie, come here."

'"Why? What more do you want from me?" I spat out.

'Knowing how upset I must be, he wasn't his usual overbearing self. With great tenderness he said, "Come close to me, Dhupi darling. Come." Once I went over, he held me close, wiped away my tears and said: "You've heard it all. I'm so terribly sorry."

'At this I began to sob: "Why did you do this to me, Thakurda? Have I ever been astray? Did you ever see me go with boys? I've always listened to my elders. Why should this happen to me? I was happily working ..."

'He said, "Listen, your sister Didi's groom was your Baba's doing. But for you, it was me who approved the match, yes? What's done is done, but I'm going to try to make it right. Here's my promise: your Baba and all are three brothers, so my property gets divided three-ways after I'm gone. I give my word that if you face any hardship at all in this marriage while I'm alive, I will divide my property in four and leave one part for you. I hope this safety net brings you some relief. Does it?"

'Relief or not, I knew there was nothing to be done. I mumbled, "Yes."'

In the event, Buttermilk didn't cash in her grandfather's insurance. She realised early in her marriage that she needed to be in charge if it was to work. 'On balance,' she says, 'my marriage could be worse.' Her man is demented, but at least he's not violent. Most men around her drink and beat up their wives. Jhoro would never do that. If he earns even fifty rupees, he brings it all to Buttermilk. If he needs money for a smoke, he asks her for it.

Her grandfather saw that she was doing fine. When he passed, his property was not divided in four.

Jhoro's disability meant that he was let off many duties men perform in rural agricultural life. For instance, his mother never sent him to the village markets to sell produce because he couldn't keep track of accounts at all. After watching from the sidelines for a few years, Buttermilk stepped in.

'Why don't you send him to the market today?' she asked her mother-in-law one morning.

'Because he'll screw up!' she replied.

'It's not enough to say that. You should've thought of this when you married off your cotton-headed son. Once a man is married, he has a family to support. If he doesn't learn to not screw up today, not even tomorrow, then when is he going to learn? Someone has to teach him!' No longer the fresh bride, Buttermilk was not holding back.

As the women sparred, Jhoro's uncle took Buttermilk's side: 'She's right, you know. You ought to send Jhoro on market errands.' The men were tired of Jhoro getting off easy.

They had planted a patch of broad beans that year. Buttermilk plucked a large basketful and sent Jhoro off to market. He was to sell the beans and get groceries with the money. In addition, his mother gave him ten rupees and an empty bottle to bring back some coconut oil. The money was tucked in his shirt-front pocket. Once at the market, no sooner had he set his basket down, he was thronged by a crowd. This was the busiest market day of the week. Everybody wanted broad beans. Someone said, give me two kilos. Before Jhoro could finish weighing beans for this customer, another asked for three kilos. That muddled him up. He tried to focus. He weighed beans and handed them out, weighed beans and handed them out. There was no room left in his head for money. And no one paid him either. They just took his beans and vanished. When his basket was empty, the question of money dawned on Jhoro. He looked around. Shoppers streamed by. He stopped them at random: 'O Dada, O Kaka, you haven't paid yet!' They turned on him, 'Pay you for what?' He said, 'You just bought broad beans from me, didn't you?' They flared up and said, 'Beans? Who's bought your beans? Here's my bag, do you see beans in it, asshole?' Those who had bought the beans were long gone. Jhoro felt completely dazed. His mouth went dry.

He slinked away from the market and went to the grocer. Presenting the empty bottle, he said, 'Dada, give me 100 grams of coconut oil.' The grocer looked up and saw Jhoro's deflated face.

'Ei, what happened to you? You look like you got run over!'

'I brought broad beans to the market. Everyone took them but no one paid.'

'Good god, what an ace idiot you are!' the man said, measuring out the oil. 'Wait until your mother hears about this. You're in for trouble today.'

Jhoro reached into his pocket to pay. No money! He was in full panic now. 'Wait, where did the money go? I know Ma had given me ten rupees!' While he was thronged and busy weighing beans, someone had picked his pocket. The grocer coolly said, 'Just leave your bottle here. You can pick it up next time.' He didn't trust Jhoro with credit.

Jhoro went home, drained and empty-handed.

When his mother heard what had happened, she flew into a vicious rage. It was all directed at Buttermilk. 'Aaaynh, she's flown in yesterday and wants to call the shots! And we are all flood debris here, yes? Didn't I say he'll screw up, don't send him? Thirty kilos of broad beans down the drain! And ten rupees besides. Take me now, thakur, I can't bear it anymore!'

Buttermilk was wrenched, but not about to give up. She said, 'He's been swindled once, he may get swindled again. But on the third go, he'll learn. You've lost some money. Fine. Here's your ten rupees.' She had some money from selling eggs. 'And the broad bean money? I'm going to get that back to you as well.'

The next day, she harvested an enormous pile of pnui greens. She weighed them and cut them up into sections, then made each section into a tight bundle fastened with banana stem strips. 'Take this pnui to market,' she told Jhoro. 'If folks crowd you, you'll say that your stuff is not for sale. You'll serve one person and take money from him. While you're serving one, if another one asks to be served, you'll say your stuff is not for sale. You'll give out one bundle and take money. Twenty-five paise each.' She had a lot of coins from selling eggs that she handed to him so he could return exact change. That day, Jhoro sold the entire lot. He came back and handed Buttermilk the money: seven rupees and fifty paise. She immediately went to her mother-in-law and said: 'Here's your broad bean money. Those people who didn't pay yesterday paid up today.' Since then, whenever she sent him to market, she would give him detailed instructions. In about a year or so, he could do it on his own without any handholding.

'When he had become an expert,' recalls Buttermilk with pride, 'my husband's uncle told my mother-in-law, "You birthed Jhoro, true. But you couldn't raise him. Today, a girl from another home is doing that job!"'

This was a particularly satisfying trophy. It occupies a special place in Buttermilk's mental scrapbook of small victories. 'I had to raise my husband, along with my three children.' She did this while learning the ropes as a rural bride herself.


'I was just giving my daughter-in-law a talking-to the other day,' said Buttermilk. 'She refuses to spend any time in the village. Can you believe it? My mother-in-law has just had her cataracts removed, so she can't do any housework. My husband is there in the village for the harvest. He's cooking for both his mother and himself, on top of working the field, poor thing. I don't even have time to die, how can I help out? The natural thing would be for my daughter-in-law to go to the village and take charge of the kitchen. But she just won't go. She says she's a city girl, she can't bathe in the pond. The pond! Am I asking her to poo in the field? No, right? We have a toilet in our village house now. I was also raised in the city. Will anyone believe the things I had to do as a new bride?'

Buttermilk's mother-in-law, as is typical in India, was an adversary. It was Jhoro's uncle's wife who folded Buttermilk into the ways of the village. 'She said, "Listen girl, you wake up at dawn and the first thing you do is soak the dirty dishes in the pond. Then go do your business in the bamboo grove. Come back and bathe in the pond, wash your nightclothes, wash the dishes and carry it all home." Much of the year was fine, but try and picture this in the winter. You take off your sari and wash it, while wearing your petticoat pulled up above your breasts. Then take a dip in the frigid waters. All the women going through the same routine, a lot of teeth chattering! After your bath, wrap the wet sari around you, wash your petticoat, pick up the pile of washed dishes and shiver home in the cold. Then there was the business of starting up the stove. We were used to coal in the city. In the village, you started the fire with straw and kindling. But there's a technique to it that needs to be learned. Baba–Ma had just pushed me off the deep end with no hints on swimming at all!'

There were other challenges. Her in-law's extended family had a single kitchen, in which five kilos of rice were cooked daily for lunch and five kilos for dinner. And three kilos of kheshari lentils. All products of their own fields. There might be an additional dish of potatoes and squash that everyone got a little bit of. But rice and lentils were the staples. Buttermilk would get spooked by that five-kilo vat of rice. She just couldn't get it off the stove. She was scared of being scalded by all that hot starch, or worse, losing her grip and dumping the rice. 'My mother-in-law would taunt me over this and I'd feel stung. So, one time, early in my marriage, I asked Ma if I could come stay with her for a month. "A month!" Ma exclaimed. "Whatever for? And what will your in-laws say?" I said: "You sent me to another home with absolutely no training.

I just want to come and learn a few kitchen tips from you.'" But Bashona was not much of a cook herself. She was far too busy working her eight homes. She did have a three-kilo vat of rice that Buttermilk practised on. Later, as she had children and her body filled out, that five-kilo vat didn't seem so scary.

The children came in quick succession. Her first birth, a daughter, was at twenty-one. 'This was the week after Indira Gandhi was killed. I remember that day. I was at Baba's village for the birth, although Baba–Ma were back in Calcutta. Kaka rushed in and said: "Don't leave the house! There may be trouble." Later in the day I heard that she was dead. No one told me how she died. I was heavily pregnant. They probably thought it'd be bad for me. There was no TV back then. Everyone just listened to songs on the radio.' Her second daughter was born two years later and her son three years after that. By twenty-six, she was a mother of three.

Jhoro worked hard, but he couldn't manage a good yield from his share of the land. 'Rice farming is not just labour, there's a lot of brain work. He couldn't plan. Or even think.' Since the extended family ate together, there was resentment brewing over subsidising Jhoro's unit. After Buttermilk's son was born, her mother-in-law started to grouse openly: 'One mouth popping up after another, three more to feed now!' She made Buttermilk take on husking jobs from the village to compensate for the weight that Jhoro was not pulling. Husk one sack of paddy and get a kilo of husked rice as pay, that was the deal. Each sack had 55 kilos. Buttermilk stayed up after finishing all household chores and husked a sack daily. 'Husking is back-breaking work. And I had to do it after minding the kitchen all day and running after three little kids. Some nights my body just gave up. I would doze holding onto the rail above the husking station, as my foot kept working the ram.' *Thunk thunk thunk*. Much like her mother husking into the night, twenty years before.

This was not all. At busy times, such as plantings or harvest, the men were often short of hands and the women had to pitch in. 'At plantings, for instance, we'd get to the fields by 4 a.m. and work for six or seven hours. You're bent at the waist like a hairpin, knee-deep in pillowy mud. You have to have a light touch—push each sapling in gently, don't twist your wrist, that'll snap the stem. And do this at a fast clip, a sapling every two seconds or so, evenly spaced.' They would work non-stop for a half-hour, then break for a brief rest on the raised aisle at the edge of the field. The men smoked bidis, the women chatted. Around them, the land was filling up, one green jot at a time, clear to the horizon. Break over, the men took their last long drags, the bright cherries as if a signal to get back into the mud.

4

# City Girl

Calcutta's slums don't collect scum-like at the city's fringes. They weave, like oil slick on water, through its neighbourhoods. Clusters of low shanties thrum with a rural rhythm, cheek by jowl with leafy streets on the urban grid. All slums are not equal, with a wide variation in location and amenities. In this pecking order, Ponchanontola occupies the top rung. Situated on train tracks, close to tony neighbourhoods in south Calcutta, near markets and all manner of work, it is a preferred shelter of the city's working poor and their families. Karno didn't know it at the time, but when he washed up here fleeing rural horror, luck had favoured him. It was a good place to raise children.

He had decided not to bring all seven of them over. He thought his elders would suffer in a house abruptly drained of children. His second son, Mejo, was the only one going to school at the time. Karno left him behind in the village to be raised by his parents. It didn't occur to him that Mejo, then just six, might be damaged by this split.

The uncle who had helped Karno settle in Ponchanontola was a well-connected man, an established firewood trader. Karno was able to quickly find work through him. He did double shifts—a construction labourer during the day, a cook at night. But even so, he wasn't making enough to feed his large family. His uncle suggested that Bashona take up work as a maid in nearby Ballygunge. Karno initially baulked: 'Washing others' soiled dishes and soiled underwear? Out of question!' No women in his family had worked outside the house before, much less as a maid. 'Little did Baba know,' adds Buttermilk, smiling as if at an endearing absurdity, 'that even fifty years later, his daughters would still be maids.' Karno got over his mental block soon enough. In a year, he had also placed his two eldest children Dada, eleven, and Didi, ten, as domestic helps. Everyone left for work in the morning. Buttermilk, the third child, was in charge of watching her three younger siblings aged two, four and six. She was eight.

This was not her only job. She had to step out to fetch water from the public faucet that came to life twice a day at specific times when the entire slum would throng it. If the line got long, she had to carry the two-year-old along because leaving her behind was risky. This naturally made carrying the water back that much harder.

The year was 1971. 'There was a war or something bad going on nearby,' Buttermilk remembers. 'The streets were full of people who had come from far away, much farther than us. They said they came on foot. They were skin and bones, their clothes were rags. They were even poorer than us.' Calcutta had become the refuge of desperate millions fleeing a massacre. In the chaos, Buttermilk found an opening. 'The neighbourhood club had begun handing out food every morning: a cup of milk and two slices of bread. My thinking was, if I could somehow get my three siblings in line, I would score four portions. So, I would get an early start and take them, one at a time, across the train tracks. I was too little to carry them on my hip. I had each cling to my chest like a baby monkey. I'd deposit the three of them at the club door like beggars and get in line. When my turn came, I'd argue ferociously: "There are four of us, you have to give me four portions!" After I got the food, we would sit there and eat together. Then I would carry them back again, one at a time, across the tracks.'

In another couple of years, Karno had found enough footing to set up a rice vend in the slum. His family of eight—he and Bashona, and their six children aged thirteen to four—lived in a room that was roughly a seven-foot cube. A raised bed covered half the floor space, about three and half feet off the ground, flush with the walls. A short bamboo ladder was propped against it for easy access. The bed slept four. The space under the bed was a crucial alcove. One corner was used for storage—dry provisions, bedding, pots and pans. The rest of the space under the bed was used for prepping meals during the day. At night, it was where the other four slept. And they all slept like rocks, as trains juddered past all night long on tracks just a few feet away.

The family's lunch routine at this point went something like this. Karno would shutter his stand and get home around 11 a.m. Buttermilk's job was to get their portable coal stove going by then. This had to be out next to the tracks so as not to smoke up their home. She also had to get the rice vat ready, measuring out cups of rice and pouring in water, as per instructions left by Karno. But she couldn't carry it out to the stove. It was far too heavy. Karno did that when he got home. He would then make a quick trip to the market nearby and bring back fish and produce. He would fry the fish and prep the vegetables. The rice is boiling by now. He takes the rice off the heat, puts on the fish and vegetable stew, and slips out for a quick drink. He's back after downing a couple, licking the leaf plate the drinking snacks were served on. He takes the fish stew off the heat, puts the rice back on and goes for his bath. By the time he gets back, Bashona is home, along with Dada and Didi. Bashona checks the rice for doneness and drains it. The family sits down to a hot lunch that Bashona serves.

Bashona was soon taking Buttermilk along on her maid shifts; this was how she acclimatised her daughters to maid work. Buttermilk was to watch and help out if she could. Fetching drinking water, for example. 'Back then, everyone had these slim-necked terracotta pitchers for drinking water. Ma would collect pitchers from the eight homes she worked in and drop them off at the neighbourhood drinking-water faucet. I would stand in line for her and fill the pitchers when my turn came. This was a tough hand-pump. I had to hang my entire weight on the handle and swing in order to move it. I would dangle and dance, such fun! But you had to aim well, you see, those pitchers have annoyingly tiny mouths. The full pitchers were too heavy for me to carry, of course. Ma would do that later. I'd similarly stand in line for her at the milk booth, with a crate of empties. Again, I couldn't carry the full bottles back. But I would save her the waiting time.'

When her periods started at thirteen, Bashona placed Buttermilk as a live-in maid, and thus began her life of paid work. She lived and worked in the city but her every move would be chaperoned. Those were Karno's rules. And you broke them at your peril. One incident stands out in Buttermilk's mind.

This was before I'd begun helping Ma on her rounds. I must've been ten or eleven. On top of babysitting my siblings, I had several household chores, such as laundry. I had to go stand in line at the public faucet to get my load done. It would take maddeningly long. One day a neighbour aunty said, 'I'm going to the Lakes for laundry. Want to come?' We were strictly forbidden to visit the Lakes without Baba. I figured I would be able to sneak a visit before he got back from his rice shop. I left my siblings with a neighbour, locked up the house, and with the laundry basket balanced on my head, walked over to the Lakes. After doing the laundry, I took a nice long bath. The water there is so lovely! As luck would have it, Baba got back before me. When he saw our home locked his first thought was that I'd gone to fetch water. But the buckets were all in place. He went to the public faucet for his bath. When he came back, I was hanging up the laundry to dry. He knew I hadn't been to the faucet for laundry.

He asked, 'Where were you?'

I froze. I knew no matter what I said I was in trouble.

The neighbour aunty who I'd gone with heard Baba growl, and hurriedly confessed, 'Bawrda, it wasn't her fault. It was me who took her to the Lakes.'

Baba swatted her words away. 'Aah, who asked you? The one who's been asked should answer!' He kept repeating his question, his pitch rising with each bark.

I broke down. In between sobs I mewled, 'Aunty said … Lakes … line was very long … so I …'

He lunged at me and began raining blows on my back. Just then

*Ma walked in, back from work. She instantly took my side: 'The girl takes care of three children. She does the laundry. How dare you hit her?' As Ma yelled at Baba, he released me and went for her, giving her a few blows. This was his way of saying: do you want to coddle the children or let me cut them to size? After hitting both Ma and me, he decreed that I was to go without lunch. Ma had set a place for me; he yanked up the mat and threw it away. He heard Ma weep while serving lunch and made to hit her again, so she stopped. She quietly stuffed me into the neighbour aunty's home. Baba ate, all my siblings ate, but Ma couldn't eat. How could she? I hadn't eaten yet. When Baba finished and went to wash up, she quickly filled a bowl with food and slid it across to the neighbour. After Baba came back he ordered Ma to eat. Feeling a bit better after having smuggled me the food, Ma was able to eat. Next door, I quietly finished my bowl.*

*I emerged at dusk, having kept a low profile all day. Baba was leaving to go to the market. Seeing me, he turned around and came up to take a close look. He had such eagle eyes! He noticed that I looked juicy enough, not pinched like I should've been if I hadn't eaten all day. He gave a grim nod and went his way. Night fell, everyone was cooking dinner.*

*My neighbour aunty ventured to tell Baba, 'Bawrda, you've punished her enough. Let the girl sleep at home.'*

*Baba flew into a rage. 'No, let her sleep with those who have fed her!' He was confident that the aunty had fed me lunch.*

*She protested, 'Trust me, Bawrda, we didn't feed her. Do we look like we can make that much extra food?'*

*It was past dinner before Baba allowed me back in and asked Ma to hand me my share of food. He couldn't yet let us eat our fill, we each had our share. Ma gave me my three chapattis. I quietly went* up the ladder to bed and stuffed the chapattis under my pillow. I planned to eat them in the morning. I used to be ravenous when I woke up, and they couldn't really give us any breakfast.

Later at night, I heard him ask Ma: 'Has she eaten her chapattis?'

Ma said, yes.

He said, 'Then ask her to come and sleep down here with you.' He was thinking of me: I've hit her, kept her hungry all day, she'll feel better if she sleeps near her Ma.

But I had stuffed the chapattis under my pillow and didn't want to get caught! I resisted going down, so he gave me a couple more blows. As I shifted downstairs, he noticed the chapattis under the pillow. 'What, you haven't eaten them?' I froze again, then told him the truth that I had saved them for the morning when I get really hungry. At this he softened. He hugged me and gave me money to buy these crunchy biscuits we used to love, shaped like pointed gourds. They were five paise each. He gave me twenty paise and said, 'Eat your chapattis now, you can have biscuits in the morning.' This is how he was. Harsh with the stick, then full of sweetness and bribes. Say he's hit you and you're sulking. He'll come and crack such a joke that you'll cramp up laughing! Big love, that's what he gave us. Nothing small about Baba.

I guess you could say he was small in stature. He was about as tall as me, which is small for a man. I'm built like him, but I've begun to balloon like Ma. Ma also had a pudgy face like mine. Baba had a clear jawline and a sharp nose. He was thin but buff, like a coiled whip ready to strike. But if you looked in his eyes, you would see a twinkle.

Why didn't he allow us to visit the Lakes? For a very good reason. When you see the Lakes today, it's all lovebirds and morning walkers. Well, back then it was a den of anti-socials. Various shades of leaf-

*smokers would hang out. Even during the day. Rapes and murders were not uncommon. I was just reaching puberty. If somebody so much as touched me, my life would be over. Baba was looking out for me. But his methods were a bit mad.*

# 5

# Monsoon Crop '14

It is early December. The city air has a nip. Not so much that the homeless are burning trash to keep warm, but enough for those living in homes to crack open their woollens. In rural Bengal, all hands are on deck for the busiest rice harvest of the year: the amon crop, planted five months before, at the first flush of the monsoons.

'Do you want to come see my village?' Buttermilk asks one morning while sweeping the floors. 'Winter is settling in. It's a lovely time!' Her face glows. What light is this? Is it the land? I wouldn't know. I'd like to find out. But she remembers something, her mouth puckers. 'Aah, but that won't work. I'd completely forgotten. There'll be bombs. And maybe even guns. I don't care if I get hurt. But if something happens to you, I'll be in a deep ditch.'

'What are you talking about?'

'I'm expecting a big row. This is how it is at every harvest. I've hired ten goons who'll show up for the first day. Their going rate is 300 rupees. I've told them I'll pay 400.'

'Ten goons?'

She laughs at my slack jaw. 'Of course! I had to. What would I do instead, stand and eat their blows? The other party has hired goons too. They'll come with scythes and machetes. And homemade bombs. We'll be ready as well.'

'That sounds like a big expense.'

'You bet! And this is only to harvest my three-bigha parcel. Just 4,000 rupees is how much I'd make by selling that rice. And there's already money sunk in it—for labour, for fertiliser. I'm not making anything. But I'm doing it for this,' she says, rapping her right foot twice on the floor. Then she furls back to her invitation: 'No, don't come now. I'll take you in February, for the next planting.'

Whenever Buttermilk speaks of her land, she seems touched by it. She goes into a trance now and proceeds to mime for me what I would see had I been to the harvest. 'This is how we do it,' she says, hitching her sari halfway up her thighs and tying its free end around her head in a bandana, 'need to deal with the mud below and the sun above!' Then, imaginary sickle at the ready, she catches herself in the act and dissolves into peals of laughter.

She has a life of the land. Land that both binds and gags.

Buttermilk's in-laws were landlords until a few generations ago when the family fell on hard times and much of their land was lost to creditors. The rest—parcels far from the village—was divided up amongst the warring factions. In 2002, when a large parcel of land came up for sale close to the village, the family collectively decided to go for a swap. Jhoro was to sell his distant parcel and buy an equivalent five bighas nearby. The seller, Dr Phoni, was a respected figure in these parts: an ageing patriarch of an old landowning family and a practising homeopath. For the land she sold, Buttermilk did all the formal paperwork. But for the land she bought, the paperwork hit a snag. Jhoro's seven brothers all got their new parcels deeded promptly by using their sale proceeds for the purchase. Not Jhoro. A younger brother needed capital for a new business he had floated. Rather than risking his own, he talked Jhoro into lending him the proceeds of his sale. He promised to pay back in instalments directly to the seller and convinced Phoni of this plan. Phoni accepted with a proviso: Jhoro's deed would only be formalised once the payment had been made in full.

'You can see what's coming,' sighs Buttermilk. 'My brother-in-law's business went belly-up after just a few instalments. That money was not coming back. I had to take over the payments. On a plain piece of paper, we kept a ledger of how much was being paid and when, which the doctor would sign each time. In a couple years, the good doctor passed. His sons took over. I kept up the payments to the eldest, Shobhon. That plain piece of paper is the only document I have for my land.'

Ten years went by. Buttermilk had paid out 70,000 rupees by then and thought she had 10,000 left to pay. She told the sellers at that point that she would clear the dues if they formalised the deed. They refused. She stopped paying. Since then, each planting and harvest brings a flurry of intimidation from the seller's musclemen, and recurrent grief. In 2013, she was approached by Tapon, the doctor's youngest son. 'He's a world of trouble. Never worked a day in his life. All he does is play with his ancestral land. He said, "Take your money and return the land." Such nerve! Can I get my old five bighas back for that price now? Don't I know how much land prices have soared in the interim? I'm going to hand him back the land and stand watching as he sells it for a truckload? I blew him off. We've farmed it all the twelve years since the purchase. Let him try and evict me.' Buttermilk knows her bargadari rights, which sustain her claim to a parcel that she has continuously farmed, even without proof of legal ownership. So she works in the city and bleeds money into working her land in order to hold on to it. 'It's a conch-cutting saw,' she says. It cuts both ways.

Amidst the planting of her amon crop in late July 2014, things came to a boil.

*Our five bighas are spread across three pieces: a low-lying three-bigha that is a perennial headache since it floods easily, an adjoining one bigha, and another one bigha that is a bit apart. When the rains opened up in earnest late June, it was time to break up the seedbed and plant the saplings to prepare the paddy field. This is a busy time. My husband went to work on the field one morning and saw three men planting saplings on our three-bigha plot! They were not from our village. My husband asked them what they thought there were doing. They said, 'We've bought this land from Tapon.' My husband went and gathered his brothers and nephews. Together they shoved the outsiders off the land. But now I was stuck. What should I do about the planting?*

*I can't go to court. I spoke to a lawyer; he said, 'There's nothing in writing. How can the law get involved?' I went to the Party office. They said, 'This is a private dispute. We can't get involved.' Tapon must've paid them off. The Panchayat office said, 'This is not our job.' The police won't even show up unless one of us is assaulted and, ideally, some blood is spilled. I finally went back to the Panchayat office and said, 'If you help me out, I'll donate five kathas for a festival ground.' So, the Panchayat pradhan called a sitting early this month. Shobhon and Tapon showed up from the seller's side. From our side, all the other seven brothers came. And me. They all live in the village, it's easy for them. It's just me who has to come running from the city. Each of these things is a day off work. But the rains are here and these saplings needed to go in. This had to get settled now.*

*At the start of the meeting, the pradhan asked the sellers, 'Whose land is this?'*

*They said, 'It was our father's. It is ours now.'*

*'Has there been a formal partition?'*

*'No.' This was important, because Tapon thinks that my five-bigha parcel falls within his imagined share.*

*'The deed has not been formalised, but there is proof that you've received payment?' the pradhan asked.*

*'Yes,' said Shobhon.*

*Tapon quickly added, 'But I didn't get my share.'*

*'That's for you to settle amongst yourself. The buyer has paid, yes?'*

*'Yes.'*

*The pradhan then asked, 'Can the same land be sold twice?'*

*At this the brothers fell silent.*

*The pradhan continued: 'Then I have to say that this is greed. You're gutting the poor. They've had to spit blood to make the payments. If there is an outstanding balance, deduct a proportionate piece and arrange to get the rest of the land formally deeded immediately.' And then he issued a grim notice. 'The men you had sent to work the buyer's land, we could've buried them right there. But we didn't. Please get this issue resolved amicably.'*

*The brothers groused, but in principle agreed to formalise the deed. The obstacle is getting their five sisters together, who are married and live all over the place.*

I was naturally happy with this outcome. But the deed gets done whenever it gets done. What about the monsoon planting? With the heavy showers we're getting now, each day before planting is a waste. The pradhan moved on this issue: 'You are trying to sell a land that has already been sold. Who has the rights to farm this land? The existing buyer, naturally.' This was a huge relief!

But the other party, the so-called second buyer, began to wail, 'What about my investment? How am I going to recoup my loss?'

The pradhan ruled, 'The labour and other costs that you've paid has to be borne by the seller.' He pointed at Tapon. 'The seeds that you've already planted, we villagers will collectively gather and reimburse you. But don't ever come back and cause further trouble.'

This was two weeks ago, mid-July. My husband went ahead and planted the saplings. And with the rainy July we've had they were growing in leaps. Then last week, an unexpected blow. My husband was out in the field when the pradhan came by and said, 'Who's asked you to work this field? Have I? Why is the doctor's family pressuring me?' He's done a complete U-turn! Apparently, one of the doctor's daughters who lives in America has asked, 'How can they farm the land when we haven't signed off on it?' They must think we move with our face buried in grass. She lives in America, what does she care if there is rice on the land or poo? That Marwari home I work at, their two daughters live in America. When they come on visits, they tell me that folks who clean homes like me in America make 30,000 rupees a month. The janitors who clean bathrooms there come to work driving their own car. And someone living in that country is going to get breathless over a few lakhs? I think what really happened is that Tapon offered the pradhan ten kathas when he heard that I'd offered him five. This America mumbo-jumbo is a smokescreen.

*I really can't continue to fight this land. With my broken husband and having to constantly run to the village to put out fires, I just can't. If they gave me even half of it in writing, I would sell it at today's price, put the money in the bank, and run the house in Subhashgram on the interest. I could get my husband day-labouring jobs. That would be a life of peace.*

*Tapon and the pradhan are closing in on me like a pincer. But I am Karno Haldar's daughter. It's not that easy to crush me. The pradhan thinks he can pressure me into upping my offer. Let him wait and stew in his greed. After the pradhan's somersault, I told my husband to pull the saplings out. We waited a couple of days and have replanted them. Things are wet enough now that the saplings didn't really notice. We will get an amon crop. But I can tell that at harvest there will be war.*


Buttermilk said she'd happily get out of her land at market price, which she assesses to be 5,00,000 rupees. That sounded to me like her ticket from permanent war to permanent peace.

'What if you got that money somehow, say as a gift?' I asked.

She looked at me like I was a slow student. 'And how would I explain that to my Subhashgram neighbours? Or in the village? We don't live like you do in these flats, behind closed doors. For us, everyone knows everything.'

I wondered if she knew about the flip side of privacy, about loneliness.

Wasn't there a way to attract a potential buyer with a suitable discount for the lack of paperwork? 'No'—she was certain—'no one in the village will buy that land. Why would they? They can simply occupy it if they could start farming.' The thought of her land orphaned had rattled her. 'No, if I walk away, that land will be gone. Another strike against me for my in-laws, who are already stung about my city living.' She was in a Gordian knot with her land, with community and family ties woven in. I couldn't fully read the braiding, but I could tell that money alone was not going to cut it. Perhaps she could use legal help.

I spoke to a lawyer friend about Buttermilk's land. He couldn't find much to work with. 'That plain piece of paper will be worthless in court.' This even Buttermilk knew. But was there no redress? 'Can you be sure of the facts? She says she has the seller's signature on the paper. Can she prove that it is in fact the signature of the man, now dead?' A valid concern. Buttermilk can't read. He added, more ominously, 'You have no locus standi in the matter. Can you prove that you don't have an ulterior motive if you take this to court on her behalf?' His only suggestion: 'She could build a small structure somewhere on the parcel. Temples are the hardest to remove. In addition to continuous farming, this would solidify her occupancy.' Which is to say, her squatting. On land that she has largely paid for.

In mid-December, Buttermilk went to her village for the harvest. She left after work on a Friday and came back, drained, on Wednesday morning. The city homes she had abandoned for those four days were bathed in wintry dust.

In addition to the ten goons, she had arranged six labourers to start work at 6 a.m. on Saturday. She arrived at the field at 8 a.m. to find the goons in place, but no labourers. No presence of the opposition either. Her overpaid mercenaries watched, bored, as she scrambled and managed two labourers. Jhoro and their son

Bonomali were already in the field. Desperately short of hands, Buttermilk waded in as well. They were harvesting their low-lying plot, which, even two months after the end of the monsoons, bore knee-high standing water. The ripe paddy rose a few feet above the water line. The golden ears drooped, heavy with grain. And the water was chilly.

The work is to stand in that water, legs planted askew in mud, bent at the waist; grab a fistful of paddy stalks with the left hand, bring in the right hand bearing the sickle in a smooth arc to slice it just above the water line, swing the left arm in a circle above the head and lay the freshly cut sheaf on the row of stubble behind you. Shift and repeat. Row after row. Done right, it is a balletic blur of arms, the left swinging more than the right, crossing paths at the cutting. If you're not careful, the paddy stalks will slice your palm. And the sheaves better line up, picking them up is a nightmare otherwise. They are too heavy to pick up after the reaping. They will dry on the field for at least a week, the stubble of stalks keeping them off the water. Once dry, another spate of labour will pick them up and place them on raised bamboo platforms, from where they'll eventually go for threshing, to release the grain that will fill the silo. But all that is later.

'I can't do this work anymore,' confessed Buttermilk. 'I had to give up after two hours. I was also worried. If I pulled a muscle, or hurt my arm, how would I do my city work? But you know, as a young bride, I used to work twelve hours at a stretch at harvest time! Up by 5 a.m., do last night's dishes in the pond, smear cow dung on the porch floors to freshen it up, pack a bit of fermented rice, grab water and toothpowder—no, we didn't always have toothpowder, we often crumbled a bit of wood coal—and head to the fields by 6 a.m. Work the powder into your teeth as you walk.

Wash up when you reach. Wade in and start cutting. And don't stop until 6 p.m., with a brief break at midday for the fermented rice. I worked like a demon back then. I can't do it now.' She added with a chortle, 'It's easier to wash dirty underwear!'

Her harvest work was hobbled on Saturday. But for the following three days, Buttermilk raised a full roster of labourers and the work went ahead full steam. It wasn't quite complete when she had to leave, having already taken four days off. As soon as she left, Tapon's musclemen showed up at the field, like hyenas sneaking around for an opening to poach a weak fawn. Jhoro called her in a panic. 'I told him: keep working, if they lay a finger on you, call me. That's when I can call the police. What else can I do?' She rushed back to the village after work on Wednesday, oversaw completion of the harvest, and caught a train at dawn on Thursday for a full workday in the city. She would keep flitting back and forth until all the sheaves of harvested paddy were safely off the field.

She took more time off in late December for the threshing and loading of grain into her silo. The sheaves of paddy drying on raised bamboo platforms are separated into bunches, their ends tied in a special knot. 'There's a lot to those bunches and knots,' she says. By now our relative positions are clear: she's surprised at how little I know about rice; so am I. This surprise is well-founded. I am a rice-eating Bengali, just like her. But my rice comes in a sealed bag from the store, like immaculate birth. She's doing her bit to demystify things.

'The planted sapling multiplies and a mature rice plant grows into a bunch this thick'—she makes a circle with her two hands, about four inches in diameter—'which we call a gaaba.' I hadn't heard this word before. 'It means fistful. But we only use this word for rice. A fistful of stalks. Now, you take two gaabas together, and tie their ends into a special knot, with a little tail sticking out.' Her hands braid the air, miming the knot. But she soon gives up. 'I can't show it to you without actual stalks. It's a really tough knot, it won't undo no matter what. It has to survive threshing. You have to tie the knot while the stalks are still green. They don't bend when dry. When the sheaves are dry, you take them to the thresher and feed them in tail-first, one at a time. There are machines everywhere now. Back when I was living in the village, we would thresh by hand. Grab a bunch by the tail, one in each hand, swing and hit the ground hard. The grains fall off.' She swings her arms, out of sync. 'It's hard labour, but you get better hay. The top of the stalk is good for cattle feed. You lose that entirely in the thresher. But then we hardly use cattle to work the fields now, it's all tractors. The bottom of the stalk, near the roots, is much tougher. That used to be for thatch, but no one thatches anymore. It's mostly used as kindling now. Here in the city, you've probably sat on it. It's what they spread on the ground for those all-night events. Covered with dhurries, of course.'


Buttermilk came to work on Christmas day, her face stricken. Her amon crop was finally in the silo after intense stress spread across six months. Amidst loading the grain she got news that her mother had died. Bashona, the rural wife-turned-city maid who had trained her daughters to work, was gone. Buttermilk rushed to her elder sister Didi's house where Bashona was staying. 'Ma was still warm,' Buttermilk said, her eyes welling up. But she couldn't stay long. There was trouble in her village. Someone had set fire to harvested sheaves drying on eight bamboo platforms near her property. 'It was a huge inferno. Think of those farmers. Six months of work! Isn't that a sin? Goddess Lokkhi lives in rice. If you eat some and get a drink of water, it cools your soul. And you set fire to that rice? They're saying, it's pati-fiksan.' Party friction. Clashes between political factions. 'But does even pati-fiksan warrant such sin? I saw the flames lick the night sky and said a silent prayer: I couldn't stay with you, Ma, but wherever you are, please watch over my grain!'

Preoccupied with her harvest, Buttermilk had last seen Bashona a month ago. 'Ma had said she really felt like some shoroo chaklis.' Crepes of rice and lentil batter, eaten drizzled with date palm sap. A winter treat. 'But it was only November, too early for sap. I told Didi: if you make them for her, I can arrange hive-broken honey. But we couldn't, we didn't …' The regret over this was cutting a rut into her. 'You know, Baba had expressed the same wish just before he died.'

This was the first time she'd spoken of Karno's death. When did that happen?

'Oh, that was nearly twenty years ago. He died in January, the right time for shoroo chaklis, but somehow we still couldn't make them for him. Ma often spoke of that. Maybe by asking for them she was giving us a hint that she was leaving too.' She was gripped in a vortex of grief, looking for a toehold. 'I've come to work. I'm walking the streets, doing my homes. But all I'm seeing is Ma's moon face and her smile. If I could sit near her, hold her hand …'

I tried consolation. She'd been a good daughter, she'd stared down challenges and made her mother proud.

This brought on a volley of sobs. 'But you know, Ma is blessed'—

she finally collected herself—'only the fortunate woman passes in the same month as her husband. In fact, her funeral in going to be on January 5th, the day Baba died.' A spasm of that old grief passes through her. 'It took us a few days to get his body from the hospital, though,' she says absently, 'since his was a suicide case.'

Suicide? Karno?

'I can't talk about that now.' Buttermilk clammed up uncharacteristically. 'It'll take all night and I'll cry a river. I'll tell you later.'

It would be many months before she did.

6

# Back to the City

I was getting snared by the fractal lanes and by-lanes in Buttermilk's story. I wanted to straighten out the main timeline.

'You've said you first came to the city at seven, started working as a live-in help at thirteen, then you were married at eighteen and went to live in the village. When did you come back to the city?'

'My eldest was ten.' So then, 1994. Her eldest was born the year Indira Gandhi was killed.

'Why?'

'To feed my three children. My daughters Rikta and Mamata were ten and eight. My son Bonomali was just five.'

Despite Buttermilk's support, Jhoro could not feed his family of five. He could manage the labour in farming, but not the planning crucial for a good yield. The grain produced from his share of the land wasn't all food. It also had to pay for his family's upkeep: clothes, supplies, social ties—all of it. He needed to borrow at planting and couldn't recoup it at harvest. His debts kept mounting. They were eating off the joint kitchen but Jhoro wasn't pulling his weight. There were frequent fights. Finally, when Bonomali was about two, Jhoro's mother called a family meeting and formally split off his unit from the joint kitchen. 'I would smell them frying fish for curry,' remembers Buttermilk, 'when I didn't even have rice for my children. You know what I'd feed them? I'd buy half a kilo of wheat flour and make a vat of very thin soup. Just like that cornflour soup I ate as a child in that year of the crab. Look,' she holds out her arm, 'just thinking about it is giving me goosebumps.' Buttermilk's skin is surprisingly alive.

When their debt had topped 8,000 rupees, Buttermilk decided she was going back to the city to work as a maid. Her in-laws flared up at this. 'Your mother may have been a maid in the city,' they said pointedly, 'but no one in our family has ever done that kind of work. If you go out and do this, you'll drown the family's honour. Our heads will roll in shame!'

This rubbed the Karno nub within Buttermilk. 'When my children—your family's children—eat thin flour soup while you eat fish and rice, where does your shame go then? Where does the family honour go? How is it dishonourable for someone to work to feed her children?' She had made up her mind to leave. Jhoro refused to join her. She said, 'Fine, you stay and take care of the children. I'm going to take up work as a live-in help.'


Meanwhile, Karno had gone back to live in the village in 1988, just before Bonomali was born. He had raised his children in the city, had married off the three eldest—Didi, Dada and Buttermilk— and also arranged his next daughter Shejo's match. After spending nearly twenty years in the city, he was tired of it. Besides, his uncle who had first brought him over to Calcutta was also heading back. That put him over the edge. He told Bashona, 'Let's go back. I just have one daughter left to see off. We can make do in the village.' His youngest daughter, Chutki, wasn't yet married. Buttermilk's two younger brothers, Mejo and Choto, weren't either. But marrying a son is easy. So they went back. Karno demolished his ancestral homestead and built a spacious house in its place. 'It was still mud-and-thatch,' says Buttermilk, 'but what he spent on it could've easily built a two-storey brick and mortar home back then. From that house, he married off my remaining siblings.'

Karno returned to the village and went back to farming. He worked hard and made enough to live off the land. Things were going well. After about four years of this, Bashona suddenly developed paralysis in her limbs one day. Karno scrambled to fund her treatment. 'Dada and Mejo never sent him even a punched coin in support. Choto used to send 300 rupees a month. But that was hardly a drop. Baba said: "My sons are not going to show up? Fine! As long as I have land, I can pay for this." So, he began selling off his land, bit by bit.' The treatment worked. Bashona's limbs held up. She was slow but could move about without help. 'But the thing that happened is once he began selling off his land, Baba couldn't stop. Some of the money went into Ma's treatment, a lot went into drink.' Karno sat back and proceeded to slowly consume his land.

Buttermilk's brothers fumed about this: 'Other than birth, what has Baba given us?'

The sisters countered: 'He worked himself to the bone at a young age to fill nine mouths. He raised you. He opened your eyes. Now it's up to you to go graze on your own.'

'Sure, that's easy for you all to say,' they retorted. 'He spent a sack of money each on your weddings. What has he left for his sons?'

*My first job back in the city was a disaster. Shanti, a young woman from my village, had found me live-in work at a home in Ultadanga, far north in the city. I left the village with her and headed straight there. I began work, but my heart felt like broken glass. That night they gave me chapattis and egg curry to eat. I couldn't even eat a bite. I was heaving inside, on the verge of tears. My children's faces were shimmering around me.*

*Shanti understood and said, 'Listen, go ahead and eat. How else will you work? Your children will be fine.'*

*I tried and ate a little bit. Maybe because of all the tears I'd swallowed with the food or for some other reason, the next day I had a severe case of the runs.*

*I got scared and told Shanti, 'I've been to the loo a dozen times already. I'm not staying!'*

*Naturally, she was a bit upset. 'I can't just up and take a day off to take you back. How will you go?'*

*I had noticed train tracks out the back window of this house. I pointed to that and said, 'Just put me on a train. I'll manage.'*

*At this she cracked up. 'Do you have any idea where that line goes?'*

*The truth is that I hadn't the foggiest. I didn't know that to get to my village from Ultadanga, you had to change lines at Sealdah.*

*Shanti said, 'You sit tight. I can't trust you on your own. I'll take you back in a day or two.'*

*But my heart just wouldn't listen. I went out on the pretext of going to the store, crossed the street, and asked a random stranger, 'Dada, I want to go to the station. Which way do I go?'*

He said, 'There's a rather long access to the station from here. Where are you going?'

I said, 'I want to catch a train.'

He said, 'Yes, but which train? Which station do you want to get off at?'

I had no idea. I went back in again and pleaded with Shanti, 'Please, I can't stay. Can you please take me?' By now I was sobbing.

She took pity on me and said, 'Okay. Wait until lunch is over.'

You know what lunches in the city are like. Cooking and dishes took until 3 p.m. She took me to Sealdah and put me on the 4 o'clock. I got off at Dhakuria and went to Choto's place. After Baba returned to the village, Choto had taken over our Ponchanontola home. I told him: 'Please Choto, take me to Baba's. From there I can manage to get back to my in-law's.' Imagine, I was raised in the city but didn't have the first clue about how to get around! All I knew was how to walk the few hundred metres from Ponchanontola to Ballygunge and back. That's how Karno Haldar raised us.

Choto took me to Baba, who was initially very upset. 'You want to go back to being a maid again? Why on earth?' He knew he'd married me into a landed family.

I said, 'You simply saw the land when you gave me away. Did you check if the man could work? Should we dig into the land and eat raw earth to fill our bellies? Working the land means paying for labour, for pesticide, for fertiliser—where will I get the money? Will you pay for the two sets of clothes I need every year? Will you pay for my children's? Then we can eat a bit more of our harvest.'

Baba realised what a deep hole I was in. He finally said, 'Fine, do what you think is best.' But I could tell how crushed he was.

I spent the night there and went back to my in-laws' in the morning. As I walked in, I found the household in its usual state *of vicious in-fighting. I was determined to get away from this. My children rushed to me and began to howl. I was crying too. We'd been apart for two nights. They wanted to go to the city with me.*

*I said, 'Okay, you want to come? I'll take you. You know, in the city, when you work cleaning homes, you get hungry and you steal a couple of biscuits and you get caught and they throw you into a drain. Then you die! Want to come?' I wanted to scare them off. I wanted a different life for them.*

*My eldest Rikta pleaded, 'Ma, I won't steal biscuits. I promise. Please take me with you!'*

*'Okay,' I said, 'but you'll have to do maid work.'*

*When she readily agreed, my heart broke, but what could I do? I took my children, went back to Baba and declared, 'You have to find a room for me in the slum. If you don't, I'll snap all ties with you. I'll camp on the sidewalk like a homeless beggar and figure the city out. You raised us in the city but you never let us out in it. You just fed us on time and sent us to work in Ballygunge homes. How am I supposed to function there? If you don't find me a room I'll go live on the street. I've decided to go work in the city and no one can stop me.'*

*Chutki was already working in the city as a maid and renting a room in Ponchanontola. Baba convinced her to let me stay with her and made it clear that I couldn't pay. So I began staying with her and started work. I couldn't be a live-in help since the kids were with me. I opted for shift work. I found a shift in one of Ma's old homes for 100 rupees a month. They were happy to have me. That led to other shifts. I then placed Rikta in a home. I had taken her to work in the morning and then gone for my shifts. She cried her eyes out and ran away that very afternoon! By sheer miracle, she found her way to my elder brother Dada's house. I traced her* there after work, worried witless. She said through tears, 'Take me back to the village, Ma, I'll be good. I promise never to ask to come to the city!' So, I took the children back to my in-laws'. But my mother-in-law flatly refused to look after them. I then went back to Baba and deposited them with him. They were a lot of work, naturally. Rikta and Mamata were old enough to help out in the household. But Bonomali was five, and a handful. And Ma was still recovering. After about two months, I could tell Baba was worn out. Meanwhile, my mother-in-law was starting to tire of the house emptied of children.

When I went to see her, she had softened: 'With all of you gone, Jhoro doesn't work at all. He just wanders about aimlessly.'

So I said, 'Fine. I'll take care of him. You look after the kids then.'

My mother-in-law took charge of the children. And I took my husband with me to the city.

He was terrified. I explained to him, 'If we don't both work, how can we rent our own place?'

'I don't know city work,' he said.

I said, 'Dada works as a construction contractor. He'll get you jobs as a labourer. Anyone can do that.'

He started working. We soon rented our own room in the slum. After treading a lot of water, I finally had a bit of firm ground in the city.

I've been working in the city ever since. My children grew up mostly in the village. I sent all three to school there. My daughters never had to do a day of maid work, thank god. But my son fell in with druggies. He's a dimwit, like his father, easily manipulated. He needed a strong hand to guide him. I wasn't around and I'm having to pay the price now. But how could I be in both places at once?

*For the first five years after coming back to the city, I worked like a maniac. My first shift would start at 5.30 a.m. and I didn't get done until 6 p.m. And this is without a commute, mind you. The children were back at the village, but my husband and I still barely made enough. We often couldn't eat our fill. But it wasn't a bad life. Chutki, Choto and I were all back living in the Ponchanontola slum. Back to our childhood streets. Back where I used to carry them like kittens across the tracks for milk and bread. And I was glad to get away from the tangle of my in-laws' family back in the village. This city work I could handle. I managed to pay off our village debts in a few years. As long as my limbs stayed supple I was going to be fine, I felt.*

*In 1999, it was Chutki who came up with the idea of buying a plot of land in Subhashgram. Her husband worked as a labourer with a contractor who had popped the idea in his head. 'You're living in cramped boxes in the slum. And wasting money on rent. Why don't you buy a plot in Subhashgram and put up a shack for now? You can always build a house later.' We didn't know anything about Subhashgram other than it being far away, somewhere between the city and my village. Someone with a one-bigha parcel there was cutting it up into two-katha plots and selling them. Two kathas is plenty of land—you can live spaciously, have a few trees, a veggie patch.*

*Chutki was very excited, but they had no money. So she asked me if I wanted to buy one of those plots.*

*I was reluctant. I said, 'I have all that land in the village. What am I going to do with city land?'*

*She countered, 'If you go back to live in the village, you can always sell this plot. Meanwhile you can stay in your own place and save the rent you're paying now.'*

*This sounded sensible.*

*Of course, I wasn't rolling in money either. But I had forged good relationships with all my employers. They were willing to trust me with advances on my salary. Just as you do. Over time, I was able to gather up enough advances from my ten homes to pay for the plot. It would take me years to work off that debt, but I had a plot of my own! By the time I'd finished paying for the plot, formalised the paperwork and built my first shack there, another three years had gone by. I was finally able to move out of the slum in 2002. I brought the children over from the village and we started living in our Subhashgram home as a family. It was mud-and-thatch then. It's brick-and-mortar now.*

*You'd think that things would be easy from here on out. But that's not the script on my cracked forehead.*

7

# Mothering

Buttermilk hardly ever speaks of her daughters. She has married them to good men who are reliably employed, lower-middle class. Rikta, thirty-three, is mother to a twelve-year-old daughter and lives in a suburb closer to the city than Subhashgram. Mamata, thirty-one, married back into the village, has finally entered motherhood after a scare with infertility. They, along with their husbands, form the support system for Buttermilk, whose airwaves are dominated by her son.

Bonomali took to smoking weed while still in the village. When he moved to Subhashgram at thirteen, the range of substances he could abuse widened dramatically. His life was largely unsupervised since one parent left for work and the other needed supervision himself. By seventeen, he was moving with a group of seasoned druggies. Buttermilk, like many Indian mothers, tried to fix this by marrying him off. Her plan backfired. A year and a half into the marriage, Bonomali was caught stealing for drug money and publicly thrashed. This and related events prompted his wife to walk out with their infant daughter, throwing him into a virulent tailspin of addiction. He spent the next several years in and out of rehab, which Buttermilk took on extra shifts to pay for. His most recent outing was in 2014. He still does drugs, sporadically. And works as a labourer when lucid.

I'd been hearing about Bonomali for years when I first met him. At twenty-seven, he was over two years out of his last rehab. He didn't have the pinched look of a long-term addict. A burly youth the colour of dark chocolate, he had his mother's quick smile. And a strikingly kind, almost cleansed, gaze. I asked if he liked to visit the village.

'Yeah, I go. When the rice flowers bloom. I go,' he said, his eyes seeking that big vista, past his small window. What about helping out in the fields? 'I've tried. But you know what happens,' he wiggled his thumb, pointed down, 'this bends and the neck breaks.' He twists in the rice sapling when planting, snapping the stem. 'It doesn't grow.' He knows what he does wrong but cannot fix it.

As we talked, Buttermilk watched me watch him, eagle-eyed: 'Could you tell what he just said?' Bonomali's speech is slurred, but not prohibitively. Buttermilk was in the hunt for my impression of her son. Damaged or not, this was her one true love.

'It's not just me,' she insists, 'everybody loves him, young and old. Even the dogs!' One benefit of Bonomali's addled brain is that he can't remember enough to hold a grudge. 'Say you've done something nasty to him and he's walking by you the next day. He'll greet you with a big smile and a "How are you? All well?" How can you not be charmed?'

In between rehabs, Buttermilk married him off the second

time in 2013. She had carefully calibrated this bride to match her son's damage. 'You'll see when you come,' she had said, 'She's fat, dark, divorced. Her face is like a rice vat. And she's practically bald.' Deadly strikes against a candidate on the marriage market. There was design behind this choice. 'She won't be able to leave. No one will take her.' When I met this wife, Rupa, I could see that Buttermilk had been unduly harsh, like the archetypal Indian mother-in-law. Rupa was chubby, but her round face had the bloom of youth, her smile sweetened by a chipped front tooth. She seemed cheerful enough in the face of her fate: a husband dim even when lucid, and the heft of a mother-in-law who also wore the pants in the family.

I met Bonomali on a visit to Subhashgram. I had joined Buttermilk on her commute home: the twenty-minute train ride south from Ballygunge station, followed by the fifteen-minute walk from Subhashgram station. Looking around her home, I saw my discarded bookcases repurposed as the pantry, with containers neatly arranged by height. I noticed the gleam on the red-oxide floors and the stainless-steel utensils in the kitchen on the porch. Buttermilk's home had a functional glow. It was impeccably kept and cleaner than my own. She was clearly getting better results with Rupa, I told her, than I was getting with her. Buttermilk chuckled at this: 'Rupa knows she'll be buried alive if I see so much as a speck of dust!' Jhoro came in post bath wearing a towel and proceeded with his daily ritual at the family's shrine. He picked up what looked like a school gong and began to beat on it. Sitting a few feet away, I could feel my eardrums flex with every strike. Jhoro turned around, wild-eyed, to measure the effect; he was clearly doing this for my benefit. Buttermilk rolled her eyes as if to say: see what I have to live with?

We were sitting on the bed in Bonomali's room. I could feel the squelch of rubber cloth underneath the duvet. Bed-wetting was one legacy of Bonomali's years of drug abuse. He also had erectile dysfunction, which Rupa had alerted Buttermilk to. And the occasional loss of rectal control. Buttermilk was determined to see her son repaired. This was yet another front in her war. By the time I met Bonomali, she'd been getting him a variety of treatments for several years. One of the reasons she had invited me home was to take a look at her son's medical records. Medical reports in India are nearly always in English. Not that it mattered to Buttermilk, who doesn't read any language. My job was to tell her what the reports said. This led to some theatre.

Buttermilk went into the adjoining room, which she shares with Jhoro, and came back with a sheaf of papers and handed it to me. 'Here, go on, read them carefully.' I read as the family watched, as if reading was a performance art. There were four pathology reports, all for Jhoro, regarding his brush with jaundice the year before. 'What!' Buttermilk was mortified. 'I could've sworn those were Bonomali's reports. I even set them aside. But,' her face fell, 'I obviously couldn't read the name on them.'

This gave Rupa an opening: 'You know,' she turned to me for support, 'she's always throwing papers away! I keep telling her not to. She's thrown out those reports and other ones besides. She also throws out old electricity bills.' Rupa has a smidgeon of literacy; Buttermilk has none. But she has rank. She didn't want Rupa to earn points. She quickly steered the narrative sideways: 'Where are Bonomali's prescriptions?' she rapped Rupa. 'You're the one in charge of those!'

Rupa began to rummage in her cabinet, a fine piece of furniture with drawers and shelves and some sliding glass. She produced pieces of paper, one at a time. All prescriptions in her name. Gynaecological advice. She was desperate for a child. Finally, a prescription emerged for Bonomali, utterly illegible, from an ayurvedic doctor. Then another from a homeopath. That's it.

The family agreed that Bonomali has had a raft of tests. But those reports, which they couldn't read, were now untraceable. I thought of all those hours spent travelling to the doctor's, waiting, seeing the doctor, getting the tests done, and borrowing, always borrowing, to meet the expense. I had a vision of being illiterate and ill in India. I felt drained. But Buttermilk had already moved on. 'That's okay,' she said, 'I have a plan. I'll take him to see a nerve specialist at Chittaranjan.' This is a hospital in Calcutta that provides quality healthcare for the indigent, where the waits are expectedly astronomical. 'All I have to do is some running around. But that's my speciality.'

Optimism, of a pathological kind, is her speciality.


In early 2015, a few months after he left his last rehab, Buttermilk found Bonomali a job at a betel nut processing factory located a half-hour train ride south of Subhashgram. Raw betel nuts arrive at the factory by the truckloads. They are unloaded and initially dried under sodium vapour lamps, then aired out in the open for several days. They are then hand-sorted by weight into three categories: light, medium, heavy. The dried and sorted nuts are shovelled into large sacks, suitably labelled. The sacks then get loaded onto trucks, which bring them to the wholesale market in Calcutta's Barabazar. The work, especially loading and unloading the trucks, was labour-intensive. Due to the unpredictable nature of the volume of nuts arriving at the factory, the workers were expected to live on-site, with little home leave. They were provided with dorms and a mess. But the lack of leave meant high worker turnover, which the management offset with attractive salary.

Buttermilk had chosen this job with deliberation. She didn't want Bonomali living at home in Subhashgram. 'If he's home, I swear, there's a long line to see him. All the wasted stoners come by, grinning, "Ah, Bonomali, you're back! Selaam!" Then there's this ancient druggie, who's usually stretched out stoned at the market, he'll come and say, "Bonomali, selaam!" Even the little kids, the up-and-coming pot-heads, they'll come by to say selaam. And it's not just the selaams. Say it's late afternoon, I hear the cuckoo's *kuuu kuuu*. It's not springtime, mind you. I see my boy's ears prick up. He heads to the window. I ask him, "What is it?" He says, "Oh nothing, I think I'll head out to the loo." I tell him, "Here's a bucket, you do it right here!" Then he gets mad at me, "I'm not going to do what you're thinking!" Like hell he's not! Did I carry him in my womb or did he carry me? They're going to lure him out with the cuckoo's call. Can I always be around to stop him? And if he leaves home, he heads straight to the drug den, and he's at it until he's rolling on the street. This is why I didn't want him home.'

The job fit Bonomali like a glove. A strapping youth and a hard worker, he was a natural for the loading and unloading work. He was kept out of the sorting, however, because he couldn't tell the difference between the weights. But he was overall a highly valued worker, well loved by his colleagues for his easy nature. And he was bringing in more than what Buttermilk made. But there was a problem.

Buttermilk and Rupa were utterly converged on one issue: the need for a child. Buttermilk, blind to the cues from the past, was certain that fatherhood would fix Bonomali. For Rupa, a child would bring a semblance of ownership over her life. After he was home from rehab, when Rupa brought Bonomali's erectile dysfunction to Buttermilk's attention, she attacked it on a war footing. 'I ran here, there, everywhere,' she says. 'Nothing worked. Finally, I went to a kobiraj.' More often than not, a kobiraj is a quack who serves a mash-up of modern medicine, faith healing and herbs. This one had a graphic diagnosis for Bonomali. 'He said, all those years of smoking drugs had burnt the nerves in Bonomali's thing, and it had shrivelled.' He recommended a daily regimen of pills, some of which were almost surely Viagra rip-offs. Rupa reported to Buttermilk that this was helping.

The problem arose a few months into Bonomali working at the factory. His colleagues began to call Buttermilk to report on Bonomali's episodic outbursts. He would mutter under his breath, say foul things about women in general, his first wife in particular. He would get restless. Sitting down to dinner, he would throw his plate away, scattering food everywhere. Moreover, his bed-wetting had worsened. Too ashamed to hang his bedding out to dry, he continued to sleep on the damp bed, which was now stinking up the dorm.

Buttermilk was certain that all of this was due to his unspent sexual energy, brought on by the pills. She had a tough balancing act on hand: she wanted Bonomali home so he could sleep with his wife, but she wanted him away to keep him out of trouble, which the factory job did. Plus, the pay was good. There was no question of stopping the pills. Instead, she made a clean breast of Bonomali's health issues with his manager and lobbied strenuously to let him come home two nights a week. His colleagues, all fond of Bonomali, found this a just demand and did their bit in advocating it. The management strung Buttermilk along with false promises and the occasional leave for Bonomali, but did not really relent. Meanwhile, Bonomali slowly spiralled out of control.

A year into his working at the factory, Bonomali's colleagues called Buttermilk to report that he jacks off in the loo and when they go in after him they are hit by a powerful stench. In addition to bed-wetting, he had developed loss of rectal control by now. And he walked around in pants with dried semen on them. Even in this state, Bonomali was a valuable enough worker for the management to not fire him. And Buttermilk was equally entrenched in her demand for weekly leave for him. Matters came to a head one day when Bonomali leaked diarrhoea on the dorm floor and casually wiped it with his foot, instead of a proper clean-up. This happened to be the spot on the floor where the men sat down for their meals. No one could eat that day.

What happened next was unusual: the manager came to meet Buttermilk at home, along with several of Bonomali's colleagues. He told Buttermilk that the factory wanted to keep Bonomali, but that she needed to get him proper treatment. He could go on unpaid leave for a few months and if his issues were resolved the factory would take him right back. Buttermilk, staring at defeat, pulled her son out of the factory.


I met Bonomali about a year later. He was living at home in Subhashgram and working odd jobs at construction sites. His symptoms had not abated. It seemed likely that at least some of them were due to long-term use of harsh, and possibly spurious, medication. Buttermilk, meanwhile, had given up on the kobiraj and was now reaching for fresh pastures: a nerve specialist.

I asked Bonomali about his drug use.

'Oh, I used to smoke the leaf. Alcohol, of course. But I've quit.'

What about the white powder?

'Oh yeah, that. I've done that a few times. But I threw up, and all night I had cinema in my head. My friend with me had the same thing. We don't do that anymore.'

And tablets?

'Yeah, tablets too.'

What about now?

'Now, I just smoke bidis. And chew tobacco. I've got this sore from chewing tobacco,' he pulled out his lower lip to show me, 'I'll quit this too.'

I could tell that Buttermilk was buying none of this.

8

# Slum Song

I walk to the neighbourhood milk booth at the edge of the Lakes for my daily fruits and vegetables. The vendors sit in a cluster on the sidewalk around the booth. One morning, I heard the green coconut vendor humming a tune. A bald and rotund man with betel-stained teeth, his voice had a rustic gravel to it. I dropped on my haunches next to him to listen, and his song poured forth:

> *Husband: Did you just steal a puff from my hookah, in my*
> *room?*
> *Wife: Oh, go to the market and pick a nice hookah for me,*
> *will you? I'll smoke my own in the kitchen at peace.*

The song went on in a folksy banter, our man singing both parts, with a dash of ribaldry. A small crowd had gathered by now. Encouraged, he stood up, took off the towel tied around his head, girded it around his potbelly with some flourish, and acted out the song. His spirit was infectious. It broke the dull thrum of a weekday morning, for vendors and shoppers alike. Then a group showed up, sweaty from their morning walk at the Lakes, and ordered ten coconuts. Our man got busy hacking his fruits open with his machete. Like a fleeting scent, the moment had passed.

When Buttermilk showed up for work, I was still in the song's bloom and mentioned it to her. 'Oh, that's Batulda,' she beamed. 'He's a good singer! I know him. He lives in the Ponchanontola slum. His father also vends green coconuts, you'll see him pedal his van through the Lakes.'

His father? The man looked like he could be sixty. But perhaps that's just high mileage.

'And they live right next to Prodeep.' Prodeep is my regular vegetable vendor at the milk booth. 'I've known Prodeep since his bare-bottomed days, you know. I even cleaned his ass as a baby.' Buttermilk chuckled. 'Now he's married, with two kids.'

Prodeep is a quiet man who had fallen rather sullen lately. I had seen him with an ugly bruise on his face a couple of weeks before. He said he'd had a hard fall. Buttermilk had a different take: 'He's been sleeping around. His wife caught him in the act and gave him a thrashing.' She then looped back to the song. 'That song, I bet Batulda was singing that for Prodeep! He's been having these fights with his wife, right? So, he's teasing Prodeep to make him feel better. Nothing like songs to pick you up when you're down.'

It occurred to me that Buttermilk was truly from here. She's been around this neighbourhood for nearly fifty years; at ten, I'm a relative newcomer.

Buttermilk keeps up with the news from the slum but doesn't get to visit it with any regularity since moving away. A visit was due; she had just learned that her elder brother was ill. Drugs had pulled Dada off his shelf as a construction contractor some years ago. He now begged for a living and stayed in the slum.

'Want to come along?' Buttermilk asked. 'You can see all the places I've told you about!'

She wanted me to have pictures to go with the stories. I had my own pictures, vivid images her words had painted, so there was some risk in this. But I wanted to see her childhood streets. And to be led around the neighbourhood by an old hand.

'Sure,' I accepted. 'It'd be good to meet Dada too.'

She baulked. 'No, I can't take you to Dada's.'

'Why not?'

'He lives in a …,' she trailed off, her hands tracing vague shapes in the air. 'No, not a good idea.'

She suggested a compromise: we would go together, she would show me around, then I would return alone and she would visit Dada. She was in charge of how much of her old life I would see.

We walked towards AMRI, a major hospital in south Calcutta. Buttermilk waved at the throbbing city around us—homes, businesses, schools, flyovers, giant billboards: 'When we first moved here, there was none of this. Nothing except the hospital, and the train tracks beyond. At night, we could hear jackals howl.' Past the hospital, we turned onto a street that was lined with middle-class homes for a while and then, as is often the case in Calcutta, morphed into a slum without notice. 'Here, this is the public faucet,' Buttermilk pointed excitedly, 'this is where I spent much of my childhood, waiting in line!' She sounded different, her voice tinny and high, like a child's. The faucet looked old; it had a cast-iron stump with a magnificent lion's head in high relief. It was set within a paved and sunken platform, about three feet long on each side, green with slime. I caught a faint whiff of urine. 'Once your turn came, you did everything—laundry, bath, filling your jerrycans—before releasing the faucet. There might be a hundred people waiting for you to finish!'

The street here was about eight feet wide. We soon turned into a hair-thin lane, dank from permanent shade, and followed it as it snaked through a dense warren of homes. In places, we had to press against the wall to let another person pass. The homes were stacked back-to-back like freight cars, about seven feet wide, with shared walls. The lane squiggled until the train tracks, where it opened out to about three feet in width. There, one door from the tracks, we stopped. 'This one,' said Buttermilk turning to me, her eyes glistened. She was seeing things I couldn't. I felt helpless, like I had failed in the role she had assigned me.

The home was locked. Buttermilk had not been able to coordinate with her younger brother Choto, who now occupied it. But I could see the insides of other similar homes: neatly appointed cubbyholes, exemplars in compact living. The home is about 7'x7'. Half the floor space has a raised bed, flush with two walls. Some homes have a TV mounted on one of walls adjoining the bed. The other walls bear furniture: hefty metal cabinetry, or even a fridge in some cases. The ceiling, about seven feet high, has a mini rafter bearing a mini fan. 'The slum had no electricity back in our time,' Buttermilk said. I pictured eight sleeping bodies packed tight on those stifling summer nights when the air feels like water. How did that work? 'Come along,' she said, 'you'll see.'

She took me to the tracks and proceeded to map out her various stories. 'Here's where I would fire up our coal brazier for Baba to cook lunch on.' A little paved patio with weeds spilling out from the cracks. 'There, see how close the market is?' It was less than a hundred feet away, bustling with dozens of stalls: vegetables, fish, meat. The air faintly ripe with rotting blood. 'Baba's rice shop was on the other side of the tracks, he would shop here on the way home.' Lunch dishes would be carried through that serpentine lane out to the public faucet. That walk was tricky after dark, so dinner dishes would be rinsed with stocked water and soaked overnight, to be done in the morning. 'And there'—she pointed diagonally across the tracks to a ramshackle structure, an incongruous pink—'that's the clubhouse where they used to hand out milk and bread. They hit me once for carrying my little siblings across the tracks. Too risky, they thought! But I still did it.' She smiled, as if at her own gritty childhood self.

We stood chatting right by the tracks. A few local trains galloped by, the breeze buffeting us, followed by a long slow freight train. Four tracks, all active. Did she ever get scared of these metal monsters passing inches from her body? 'Scared?' Buttermilk laughed out loud. 'This is where we hung out! You've seen the homes, there's no room to stay in. And there was no fan to keep us cool either.' The tracks were the sprawling social space where lives were aired, laundry dried, and much more besides. 'In the summer nights, this is where we all slept. We would drag pieces of cardboard from home, place them over these stone chips and put a sheet on top. And at dusk, here's where we would all sit and shoot the breeze, our legs splayed out on the tracks.

We would hear the train blare its horn while still at the Lakes and take time drawing up our legs. After the train whizzed by, we'd splay them out again!' The old glee bubbled up in her and burst out in a hoot.

I watched Buttermilk wander her memory map. She looked unfamiliar, lit from within. Showing this light to me seemed like an act of confidence. Maybe she thought I'd know what to do with it.

We were attracting some attention. Buttermilk deflected most of the curious passers-by with, 'Oh, she's my Didi.' Didi is what she calls me—literally elder sister, but in this case, code for employer. Tourists visit India's slums, employers rarely do. Unless there's been trouble. Buttermilk's response therefore aggravated the curiosity. She seemed to savour it, unwilling to share the visit with all and sundry.

One woman stopped when passing by and did a double take. 'Oh, it's you!' She grasped Buttermilk's hands with warmth. 'It's been so long! You haven't been back since your Ma passed away.'

Buttermilk introduced us. 'This is Sheela, an old neighbour. And this is my Didi. She wanted to see where I grew up so I've brought her.'

Sheela pulled us towards her home. 'You have to have a cup of tea.' It was across the lane from Buttermilk's place, right by the tracks. These end units had a real window and were therefore more open to air, and noise. I noticed this one had a vertical extension, with a flimsy balcony housing at least a dozen coops that brimmed with white fantail pigeons. I was struck. These birds—all exuberant tails and feathered feet—are preening showboats. Breeding them was once a pastime of the addled sons of Calcutta's decrepit feudal families. What were they doing in the slum?

Sheela had followed my gaze. 'That's my son's doing,' she exclaimed. 'He drives me crazy with his birds and animals!' Sheela was short and lean. Her leathery face and gap-toothed smile showed an ease hard-earned, a river off the mountain on the calm stretch. 'Do you know he's got a dog now'—she turned to Buttermilk—'one of those fluffy things that yaps its head off. The name's Lisa. Guess how much he paid for Lisa: 15,000 rupees! He came to me for it, I said: no way. So he bought it with his own money!' Her exasperation was a thinly veiled pride in her son's ways. Her son, Raja, was twenty and in college. Where did he get the money? 'Oh, he wasn't sitting idle after his board exams. He hopped from one catering job to another and had saved up quite a bit. But all that went into buying Lisa. Now who'll pay for her upkeep? Me, who else.' There was more. Raja had just celebrated Lisa's birthday the day before. 'I cooked pulao, meat curry, rice pudding—all of it. I had to, he won't take no for an answer. Thirty-five guests! They ate in batches, at both levels. And that was at dinner. During the day, he brought home a huge hoard of street dogs, about twenty. There's a ma'am on the other side of the tracks who'd given him money to buy meat for the dogs. He bought the meat, asked me to cook a large vat of rice, and fed meat and rice to the street dogs. Can you believe it?' She couldn't hold on to her mock agitation for too long, her love broke through. 'As a child, he would often ask his teachers: can I please stick to birds and animals in my studies?'

Sheela is only a few years younger than Buttermilk, but her arc has been very different. She has a high school degree that she has been able to monetise by tutoring children in the slum. 'I've been doing this for twenty-five years. I take in kids aged about ten to twelve. At some point I had over twenty. I've now cut back to ten. I used to teach them everything. But I can't do their maths anymore. They've changed it all, you see.' Her husband is a peon at a private school. They have family back in the village, but their land ties are slack. They bought their shack for 10,000 rupees in the late '90s, roughly when Buttermilk bought her plot in Subhashgram. 'We had bamboo-rattan walls and terracotta tiles for roof back then,' Sheela remembered. 'One time, I was sitting on my bed and a few tiles caved in just a hair away! Ouf! We made this into brick-and-mortar about ten years ago.'

'I had also considered buying in the slum,' Buttermilk said, 'but my brothers discouraged me. Who knew things would get so developed?'

Much has changed in Ponchanontola since Buttermilk's time. Where one faucet had served the entire slum with scheduled water, now dozens of faucets dot the slum, with water round the clock. There are proper toilets now, one for every ten homes. The streets, even the hair-thin lanes, are paved and no longer get waterlogged in the rains. The slum now has electricity, and importantly, street lights. The train tracks used to be a den for drugs and illicit liquor after dark, not anymore. But more than the civic amenities, the change is in the residents.

Educating her children was Sheela's top priority: her elder daughter Paromita has a college degree, her younger daughter Moumita has a master's degree, and her son Raja has begun college. Paromita fell in love while in college with a boy, also from the slum, polite and employed, but not a Bengali. To get around this, they eloped and got married. They live just across the tracks and Sheela gets to enjoy her toddler grandson. Paromita gives art lessons to children in the slum. In Buttermilk's era, most mothers here were maids and their daughters began maid work as early as ten. Now, the slum was home to parents who wanted their children to have not just maths and science but also art lessons.

We had settled in Sheela's home: she and I sat cross-legged on her bed while Moumita made tea. Buttermilk sat on a low stool at the doorway, her gaze occasionally flitting to the locked door across the lane. 'Just being able to sit here and chat is bringing me such peace,' she said. 'I've been close to tears all this time, thinking about all the gone people.' The women reminisced about Bashona's final years, when she mostly stayed with Choto. Being right across the lane, Sheela had more contact with her than Buttermilk did. 'She would come to me like a little kid and say: "O Raja's Ma, I really feel like some noodles!" Or, "Do you have any more of those chocolate biscuits?" And I'd happily meet her demand!' This story made Buttermilk tear up. The women switched to talking about their sons, evidently a favourite topic.

'Everybody loves Raja, dogs and humans alike, because he's nice to everyone,' said Sheela.

Buttermilk responded, 'Raja is just like my boy. In the good and in the bad.'

Raja, like Bonomali, was a well-loved youth with a drug problem. 'He was a fair and beautiful child, like a prince.' A sigh heaved out of Sheela. 'That's why I'd given him the name. Now, with the drugs and the running around, he looks like weathered bamboo. So, we tease him and say: we'll call you Proja now.' Raja is Bengali for king, proja for subject. 'But you know, just last month, a bunch of white folks showed up to talk to Raja. They had a big camera, and a long pole with a microphone,' Sheela recalled, a bit giddy. 'They kept wanting to chat with us! Do we know that much English?'

Moumita explained that National Geographic was doing an episode on Indian slum life. Their stringer in Calcutta had connected with Raja on Facebook, decided his obsessions might make good TV, and led the crew to Raja's home. 'They followed Raja around the slum and filmed our home. If the episode airs, they'll let us know.'

She delivered this bit of striking news with indifference. There was a calm luminosity in her, a lunar gravitas. An attractive woman, about twenty-five, she wore a kurti and three-quarters. Her shins were shaved to a mirror finish. When she brought me tea, I saw her nails were manicured, with a subtle shade of polish. The contrast between her demeanour and her mother's could not be greater. She knew all about National Geographic's gaze—'slum people like us' is how she put it, using English words, when explaining what the episode was about. She was not incensed by it, just a bit bored. She was born in the slum, went to the K-12 school at the edge of the slum, got a bachelor's degree in philosophy from a good college nearby, then a master's degree from the university, and now worked as a physician's assistant at a leading hospital in south Calcutta, a short commute away. She works on a computer all day, in an air-conditioned office, dealing with patient records and tracking blood samples. Then she comes home to her cubbyhole in the slum, next to the tracks. National Geographic had picked up on her brother's eccentricity, but not her patient work of transcending the slum while staying aware that she was of it.

Moumita had left me a bit tongue-tied. 'You'll be married

soon and move to a different setting, maybe a larger place,' I said. 'Do you think you'll miss this intimate living, the dense social network?' The question sounded tone-deaf, even to me.

'No,' she said, holding my eyes in a cool gaze. 'And I want to see my parents in a larger place as well. I'm working on the separation. Once that comes through, only then will I think of marriage.'

She used the English word 'separation', a code in the slum for moving away. A separate home, not this boil growing on the side of the tracks.

I later found out that Moumita was not an exception. Buttermilk's brother Choto raised two daughters just across the lane from her. The older, Rakhi, is twenty-one. She has a bachelor's degree in commerce and is studying for her master's degree while working part-time at her father's textile business. She doesn't get paid; Choto has advised her that she's investing in her inheritance. He has a successful business and has built a spacious home in Narendrapur, a southern suburb, the top floor of which houses his factory. But he preferred living in the slum because of the convenient location. Then, two years ago, he forced his family to move to Narendrapur. The reason: Rakhi was in love. 'The boy looks like a langur,' deadpanned Buttermilk, 'and works as a construction labourer.' A big step-down for Choto. He tried to dissuade Rakhi, verbally at first, then with the stick. Nothing worked. Even the move wasn't effective. Rakhi continued to see the boy in the face of all manner of threats. She confided in Buttermilk: 'Aunty, I know he's ugly and unskilled, but it is him I love. I'm going to make him stand. I won't be able to build a life with anyone else.' She held her ground and eventually married him.

I imagined other young women in the slum, blooming in cramped quarters, tending to similar reserves of strength.

9

# Village Vein '15

id-January is the peak of Calcutta's fleeting winter. The
temperature drops just enough to release a plume of
vibrant woollens out of mothballed closets. The light takes on a
sweet sparkle, more inviting for a change than shade. And in that
wintry sunlight, within each date palm all over rural Bengal, the
sap deepens to its richest bouquet.

Buttermilk came to work one morning and handed me a bottle,
one of those plastic empties best discarded after its contents are
drained. She had filled this one with liquid gold, as runny as water.
This was poyra gur: fragrant date sap just a boil beyond what's
tapped out of the palm, before being further cooked down to
stringy molasses or solid cakes. 'Here,' she said, 'why eat store-
bought sweets when you can have this, fresh from my village. My
harvest money is in!' She was celebrating the closing of her stressful
monsoon harvest that had come off the fields in December.

Date sap is sweet, yes, but that's the least of it. The thing to do
this time of year is to take a lick and wait. The reward is a subtle

chorus of flavours, salt to caramel, in a slow bloom on the tongue. I watched her watch my bliss, her face a swirl of happy and sad. Was she sad because of her mother? Bashona's funeral had been only ten days ago. 'No,' she sighed, 'it's not that. I'm here working, but my mind is stuck at the village courtyard. It's Mawkor Shonkranti today. And I can't be there. I've taken too much time off already.' Her gaze was fixed in the middle distance. 'The women have woken early, bathed, and are now making floral patterns on the floor with rice powder.' She was in a reverie. 'The house is full of guests. And the kitchen is humming with all sorts of sweets in progress.'

Mawkor Shonkranti, an auspicious date on the Bengali calendar that falls mid-January, is the time of Bengal's main harvest festival: nawbanno, literally new rice. The monsoon harvest gets packed away by this time; some of the paddy is sold, the rest husked for home use. The farmer flush and the weather clement are fine ingredients for a rural festival. But this one is also blessed by the land's seasonal largesse. The date palms brim with sap, the coconut palms are heavy with fruit, there's plenty of crushed rice at the bottom of the husking bowls. These are the chief ingredients of the stream of seasonal sweet treats that emerge from the festive kitchen. Pithey (steamed rice cakes), pooli (stewed sweet potato dumplings), patishapta (stuffed crepes), payesh (rice pudding) and much more. At the heart of the celebration is the new rice, consumed in various forms. But first, it is worshipped.

'We call goddess Lokkhi to come sit on the rice,' Buttermilk recounted the ceremony, 'and we urge her to stay.' The winter fields in between rice plantings are chequered with crops bearing blossoms in vivid hues: taxi-yellow of mustard, hot fuchsia of radish. These flowers are braided with ears of golden paddy and tied at strategic spots in the house: the door knockers, the bolt on the grain silo, the husking post, the handles of steel trunks—stations where the goddess's presence is sought. As they tie these little braids, the women chant a ditty for the goddess:

> *auni bauni kothao na jao*
> *ghawrey boshey tin din pithey bhat khao*
> (come and sit, don't you go away
> eat steamed cakes and rice at home for three days)

A bowl is dug into the mud floor in front of the grain silo and fresh paddy poured into it for worship. 'We even call a priest. It's a full-fledged pujo, you see. We offer all the pithey and pooli to Lokkhi, who's now in that pile of paddy, and eat them later as proshad.' The leftovers of the goddess. 'We fill a pitcher with paddy and set it aside for her on a loft until May.' The intention is to cover the goddess's food needs until the following harvest.

Buttermilk had sent Jhoro to the village in her stead. 'How can we both be absent for an important household pujo like this?' But as a side effect, her Subhashgram home was drained of festivities. 'Before coming to work today, I'd asked Rupa to make some pithey, but then I called and cancelled. Who's going to eat them?' she said, sounding deflated. 'Even Bonomali is gone on a construction job.' There was more. Two days before, when the fresh sap had arrived from the village, Bonomali had lobbied Buttermilk for his favourite winter treat: shoroo chakli, the thin crepe that Karno and Bashona had both wished for on the eve of death. Bonomali had made a reasonable demand: make the crepes while there's such sublime sap on hand to drizzle them with. But Buttermilk couldn't. 'Where will I find the time, you tell me.' The failure was cutting her up. 'To do it right, you have to hand-grind the rice on a mortar and pestle. Even if I had machines, I wouldn't use them. You have to soak black-eyed peas overnight and hand-grind that, which is a sticky mess. Then you mix the two into a thin batter, ladle onto a hot griddle, and quickly swirl it out into a disk with the stem end of a brinjal. No flipping. It cooks in less than a minute. You have to work fast.' It did sound like a lot of work. 'But when done right it is wonderful,' Buttermilk sighed. 'You drizzle the soft side with poyra gur, fold in half, and there's a slight crunch when you bite in.'

There was a silver lining: a tiff that Bonomali had had with his wife Rupa over his crepe wish. 'Rupa said: I'll make you some milk pooli instead, that'll be equally good. Bonomali shot back: you are a city girl, what do you know about village eats?' Buttermilk chuckled, mimicking his outburst. 'The poyra gur this time of year is in a different league, it must be paired with shoroo chakli! And Rupa wasn't backing down. So, they kept going on and on, back and forth!' Her sorrow in her maternal failing was marbled with pride. She had raised a son with land roots, one who preferred his mother's crepes to his wife's dumplings.

'My low-lying three-bigha I usually plant with fat grain,' Buttermilk filled me in on her harvest. 'They like to be wet. I put skinny grain on the other two bighas.' Fat and skinny grain? I knew nothing about this. 'Ohoho,' she clucked. 'I keep forgetting that. See, there are many strains of rice. Used to be in the hundreds, not so many now. The skinny one I raise is Dudhershawr, a fine-grained rice that city folks like you eat. It fetches a good price.' We had never discussed this but she was absolutely right. Dudhershawr is indeed the rice I usually buy. 'The fat grain is Morichshali, it is practically a sphere. Mainly used for moori.' Moori is puffed rice, which I knew came from some sort of paddy, but I had not considered its character. 'You can cook Morichshali as rice, it takes more fuel to soften. But you know, we village folks can't handle the skinny grain that you eat. Say I eat rice at two o'clock, I'll be hungry by four. My tummy will squeal like a puppy! And in the village, we are large hordes, we eat mounds of rice. Skinny grains would never work. Fat-grained rice sticks and tides you over until dinnertime. But since we don't live in the village, both the grains I raise are for selling. Otherwise, I would plant a different fat grain for eating. Heeramoti, for instance, is fat but very fragrant, and cooks faster than Morichshali.'

I was getting drawn to Bengal's rice calendar, a steady boil of planning studded with intense bursts of activity whose plumes don't reach the city. 'You have to first understand the land,' Buttermilk explained. 'Mine, for example, is tey-phawshla.' Such land can support three rice harvests in a year, the highest grade of fertility. 'But for three harvests you have to be there full-time and work at full strength. I can't be around and my husband's broken. So, we usually only do the amon.' Amon, the monsoon crop planted in July and harvested in December, is the least demanding. 'Due to my land troubles, I've taken to also doing the boro lately, to strengthen my tilling presence.' Boro is the winter crop, planted in February and harvested in May. Unlike the monsoon crop, it is not watered by the heavens. It demands planned irrigation and nutritional support, and often has an inferior yield. 'It's a load of trouble, but at least it's not as finicky as the aus.' Aus, planted in May and harvested in July, is the most labour-intensive and the speediest of the three crops. 'It fetches the best prices, about three times that of amon, but it has no coping skills. I want standing water'—Buttermilk fluttered a limp arm to mime a picky rice plant—'but not too much! Then there's the cost, because you're planting at the height of the summer heat. By the time the rains peak, your crop is ready for harvest. Or washed away by floods, if that's your fate. I tried it one year and took heavy losses. Never again.'

Now that the amon harvest was done, what was next? 'The boro seedbeds are being prepared now. We set aside some of the amon paddy as seed grain for next year's plantings, both boro and amon. But you can't just scatter dry grain and expect them to germinate,' explained Buttermilk, 'they need to be woken up. You soak the seeds, stuff them in a moist gunny sack, wrap it all with dry straw and place a heavy weight on the bundle. Then leave it for two days.' The primed seeds are scattered on compact plots that have been tilled into a moist richness. By early February, just before the boro planting, the countryside is dotted with electric green patches—seedbeds packed with saplings—within vast swathes of brown, the paddies prepared to receive them. 'Those paddies have had a lot of work done.' Buttermilk counted them, 'The straw stubble from the last harvest removed, the soil turned once, fertilised and watered, and turned again. We used to till with a plough hitched to oxen before, but now it's all tractors. And those tires leave huge ruts! The replanted saplings need standing water, those in the ruts would drown. So, we even things out by dragging a bamboo ladder.'

Buttermilk had not forgotten her invitation: she was going to take me to her village for her boro planting. 'I'm calling them every day.' She sounded flustered. 'The problem is the mobile pump unit. See, it moves from parcel to parcel on its own schedule. It will pump water from my own pond onto my land, but I have no control on when. As soon as the pump comes by and the second turning is done, we'll be ready to go. You'll get a day's notice,' she said in mock warning, her excitement palpable. Then she added: 'We'll go stand on the raised aisle as they plant. I was in a pinch at the December harvest and had to wade in. Ouf! Not this time.' This time, she would go as the mistress, to oversee her farm.

'I've told them, two people are coming.'

'Who?' I asked.

'Why, you and me.'

The signal she was waiting for came mid-February.

I sat on a mud porch eating an elaborate lunch: fried brinjal, fried fish, lentils cooked with fish head, fish braised in tomatoes and onions, and rice. A small elderly woman hovered, pressing me with food: 'Here, have more brinjal, we just picked them this morning.' In a white cotton sari and soda-bottle glasses, she was a mild and affectionate presence. This was Shashuri, Buttermilk's mother-in-law and one-time nemesis. She had prepared this feast for Buttermilk's guest at her behest, and now served it as Buttermilk watched. The power centre had shifted but left no trace of bitterness. There was ease in Shashuri's rheumy eyes. Her leathery face was creased with a smile. She served Jhoro and me, the man and the guest. The women would eat later. We sat cross-legged on embroidered jute mats and ate off heavy bell-metal plates. Jhoro ate with speed and gusto. He looked up just once. 'That rice,' he said through a mouthful, pointing at my plate, 'that's our new skinny grain.'

I was eating a farmer's work, in his presence. Attention was the least I could've offered. Instead, I was eating rice as always—as the backdrop, never the star.

Buttermilk's village is at the edge of the Sunderbans, about three hours south of the city. Half of that we had spent on the train, another hour on a rickety trekker, and the rest on foot. Her home was smaller than I had imagined, as places built with borrowed memories inevitably are. The lower level had two rooms fronted by a narrow porch, part of which was the kitchen. There were two rooms upstairs, accessed by a decrepit gangplank, which even the elderly Shashuri tackled like a mountain goat. This was half the house; the identical other half housed the family of Jhoro's younger brother. The one who had ruined him.

After lunch, Shashuri chatted with me as Buttermilk listened in. She had come to this household as a bride at seven and was now seventy. Her life and its many hardships she narrated with a lightness, as if they were not her own. She praised Buttermilk for all her work within and outside the home. Then she turned to the importance of taking care of oneself. 'The body,' she said with deliberation, 'is like that sari you wear on rare occasions.' Meaning that if you looked after it like one, it would serve you that much longer. I found this a striking code for a rural woman to live by, given that her body gets wrung out through maximal use. She sounded like an evolved soul. I mentioned this to Buttermilk as we headed out to the fields. 'See, it's like what happens to milk,' she chortled. 'Boiling milk, that's what she was in her prime. All bubble and splash. I got countless blisters. And now? Now she's cooked down to kheer! Cool and sweet. Maybe,' she added with a hoot of laughter, 'that'll happen to me too!'

Buttermilk walked me through her large veggie patch overflowing with winter produce, and past her pond stocked with fish. 'I'd meant to ask my husband to net a few for lunch today,' she said fretfully, 'but with this planting hassle now, I completely forgot!' We cut through the village. The houses were thoughtless jumbles of unplastered brick set within shady groves of fruit trees. The still afternoon air was dense with the perfume of mango blossoms. Soon, the shade and the scent abruptly fell away. We were out under a big sky, rice paddies stretching clear to the horizon.

Buttermilk kept running into familiar faces, and each time we did the ant routine: stop, chat for a bit, and go our way. 'Who's this?' was the natural question, directed at me. The first few times, Buttermilk said: 'I work in her home.' But soon this changed to: 'She's my sister, she lives in the city.' I had chosen to wear a faded cotton sari, so as to not stand out. Did that help Buttermilk say this, or feel this? Perhaps she had read my gesture as pure solidarity, missing the calculation in it. For years afterwards, she would fondly recall this walk: 'Remember that day when we roamed around the village and paddies like two sisters?'

I followed Buttermilk along a raised path; the paddy fields on either side were abuzz with activity. 'Look,' she said, 'here's a seedbed being broken.' A few men and women were clearing a dense patch of vivid green saplings, each a tuft of narrow blades about a foot tall, and bundling them for transport. 'You grab a gaaba of saplings.' A fistful. 'Gently loosen the roots. Tie two gaabas together in a bundle with a rice blade. Not too tight or you'll snap a stem and finish that plant.' These bundles, about fifty saplings on average, are then strung on bamboo yokes and transported to the paddy for replanting.

Shortly, we arrived at her land. 'Here we are! Here's my ditch,' she cried, 'my infamous low-lying three-bigha!' Six men worked an acre of land, standing in shin-deep water. Bent at the waist, each held a fistful of saplings and pushed them in one at a time, evenly spaced, about eight inches apart. At planting, the hand went under water, but its flick suggested soft mud underneath. We stood on the raised aisle, watching the men work with great speed, in a mechanical rhythm. The lead man had questions for Buttermilk. She responded with an easy gravitas. She was the mistress, supervising work at her top-grade land.

Standing next to her, I thought of her carrying this within her while doing my floors on her knees.

In a freshly planted paddy, a rat snake about seven feet long had raised itself on its muscular tail. It was over three feet off the waterline when another one, equally long, twined up along it. They stood briefly, a glistening rope of gold and black, the ageing light glancing off their wet bodies, then fell on the water with a loud thrash. They rose and they fell, intertwined their necks, looked each other in the eye, twisted into tight, parallel curls, and rolled their tails showing their white underbellies. Buttermilk and I stood entranced. 'This is a good omen,' she whispered, as if she might be overheard, 'witnessing their mating dance!' The snakes had mussed up the well-made rice bed, like lovers might a real one. But they were in fact rival males, locked in a territorial wrestle.

We ran into this striking scene on our way back from the rice fields. It was dusk now. Buttermilk got a worker to pluck a large bagful of broad beans, tomatoes, green chillies, radishes and brinjals. This was going back on the train with us, some for her guest and the rest for her Subhashgram home. On our way out, Buttermilk stopped by a relative's home. Jhoro's aunt was amidst making puffed rice from the family's Morichshali grain. The spherical grains, a few millimetres wide, had been lightly toasted beforehand. She sat at an adobe stove, a smooth rise off the mud floor, with a wok full of sand singed to a tarry black. She grabbed a fistful of grain with her left hand and tossed it onto the sand. With the murmur of a drizzle on a canvas tent the black sand came alive with white dots. She scooped up the popped grain with a colander in her right hand, shook out the sand and tossed the puffed rice into a basket, while tossing in the next fistful of grain with her left hand. All in one fluid arc. Buttermilk offered me a handful, still warm. The taste was surprisingly full-flavoured, the crunch robust. 'Different, no?' Buttermilk asked, reading the answer in my eyes. 'We can't eat the store-bought stuff. It's bland, like eating air.' I was plied with a bag of freshly puffed rice, so I could avoid eating air, at least for a bit.

Nightfall was abrupt, like a hefty curtain. It was pitch dark by the time we left for the station. The trekkers had stopped plying. Our transport was what is called a *machine van* in these parts: a motorcycle front rigged with a flatbed on four wheels. Buttermilk and I huddled on it, with six other passengers, as we juddered through the February evening countryside. A dagger wind cut right through my shawl. The headlight attracted bugs that slammed into our faces. A child next to me cried out: 'Aaaynh! Something just got in my ear!' Buttermilk, maternally, covered my ears with the end of my sari. I thought of her doing this commute several times a week during the December harvest. I thought of the women of her family who had come out to bid us goodbye. Shashuri had held me with warmth and insisted that I return. I looked over at Buttermilk. In the play of light and shade, her face was serene. She was going home, not leaving home. She had escaped the village without giving it up.

The night train back to the city was nearly empty. The dozen or so women in our car seemed to all know one another. They were mostly city maids like Buttermilk, with active rural lives, taking a late train home to the suburbs after village business. One woman was an exception: a middle-aged chocolate massif who had boarded with an amorphous bag. She lived in the village full-time and was going to the city to visit her married daughter. She described her day: she had worked on a sack of paddy—fifty-five kilos—boiled, dried, husked, chaffed. 'I cooked lunch and dinner in between, of course. Not to mention chopping hay for cattle feed. I also made some pithey and pooli for my daughter,' she pointed to her bag with a smile. 'I've fed everyone this season, except her.' Her audience murmured in admiration, laced with a distinct relief. 'Babbaah,' Buttermilk exhaled. 'I had that routine once. Couldn't do it now. And wouldn't want to!'

The women had warmly included me in their circle. But listening to them, their land ties on taut display, I felt bereft. I did not belong with them, my limp cotton sari notwithstanding. As we approached Subhashgram, Buttermilk began to fret: 'Will you manage alone?' She was going to get off, and I would continue on to Ballygunge. 'Give me a missed call when you get home,' she insisted. The car emptied out at Subhashgram. I carried on alone towards the city lights.

# 10

# A Non-state Actor

The assembly elections were around the corner, the season when the poor abruptly become interesting to the state. It was raining quid for the upcoming quo at the ballots.

'They're handing out rice,' Buttermilk declared with a knowing smile. 'Two rupees a kilo, thirty kilos per family per month!' Her smile was indulgent, like when you submit to a little boy covering his eyes to trick you into believing he's invisible. 'When they give, we take! Now it's Trinamool. Back in CPM's time, do you know what they handed out once before a vote?' Trinamool is the centre-left party now in power in Bengal after upending, in 2011, a thirty-four-year communist regime led by the CPM, the Communist Party of India (Marxist). 'A full 2,000 rupees per voter! Imagine, 2,000!' She shook a V made of two fingers, her awe at the number barely contained. 'We didn't get any, of course. My husband is a dimwit and I'm never home.' Sops of this nature are usually a blink-and-you-miss-it affair, the publicity being where the mileage is. 'Trinamool, CPM—it's all the same. They'll feed us a set menu the night before the vote. Mutton curry, pulao, ice cream.' A feast, luscious and rare. 'If you feed me, I'll eat, why not? But when I go in to vote, how will you know which button I'll press?' she asked, her eyes twinkling.

I felt a stab of optimism, foolishly as it turned out. I asked her if she knew why she had chosen the button she was going to press. 'Of course I do,' she retorted, a bit indignant. 'Our village elders decide for us, and we all vote accordingly.' Buttermilk, like hundreds of millions of Indians like her, routinely exercises her franchise, but her vote is not her own. It is decreed by marshals in her community who read the surrounding political currents, and whom political agents use as pressure points for en masse vote yields. All of this is informed by a hard-boiled survivalist give and take in which individual choice is an effete concept. And not falling in line inordinately expensive.

Whatever her feelings about the meaning of her vote, Buttermilk's opinion of the state was decidedly dim. 'Let me tell you about this two rupees-per-kilo rice,' she began. 'They're handing it out to everyone, those who have a lot and those who have nothing. Now, thirty kilos lasts only ten days for my family. The rest of the month we're eating our usual rice, yes? The price of that rice has caught fire. Why? Because the trucks that normally carry rice to the markets are tied up distributing this mountain of two-rupee rice. So the wholesale rice dealers are having to pay extra in transport to bring in their usual load. And are they going to pay that difference out of pocket? Of course not! They're taking it out of mine. So, the government is spending all this money, and I'm not saving any. What's the point?' She would make an effective advisor, if she had the time. 'And they're saying they'll keep giving this for six months!'

Rather than this festive rash every few years, she wishes the state was a somewhat steady presence. One that, if not helpful, at least didn't get in the way. Like it did, for instance, when she was settling down at Subhashgram. 'For the first few years, I had a mud-and-thatch structure that would invariably collapse by the end of the rains. One year, it had tipped over as usual. When it had fallen the year before, someone from the party office had taken 300 rupees from me, otherwise they wouldn't let me repair my home. When it fell again this year, I started repairs and they stopped the work. I rushed over to the party office. There, a grizzly old man told me I needed to give him 1,000 rupees. I said: "I just paid 300 last year! We're poor, and you can see the state my home is in. Where can I get that kind of money?" You know what he said? "You need to give something to get something." It made my skin crawl! I was still a young woman. You're old enough to be my father and you drop such an ugly hint? Taken one way it means one thing, but taken another way doesn't it mean something else? All my blood ran up to my head. I exploded: "You rotten son of a whore! Your tongue will become a pus balloon and fall off! Go, I won't repair my home. You just watch, I'll sleep out in the open with my kids!" As I left the office, fuming, the man called me back: "O Bonomali's mother, come back, listen to me. I'll send Pintu, a party boy. Give him 500 rupees. He'll give you a yellow slip. Bring it in and it'll all be fine." So, the 1,000 came down to 500. That's how it went, every year, for seven years, until I was able to build my pucca home.'

That was before. She was dealing with a different challenge now. Her Subhashgram property attracts two separate taxes: the municipal tax levied by the city and the land tax levied by the state. The sums of money are small but the paperwork is a bear. These two branches of government don't talk to each other. When a property such as hers changes hands, the buyer is required to mutate it in her name, separately, for these two entities. The process can be hairy even for the literate. For her, it is a dark tunnel swarming with unscrupulous touts. What the tunnel asks of her is not just money but also days off work. Buttermilk has given this a benign label, perhaps to take the sting out. 'I have to do a bit of walking,' she says, whenever she's dealing with government paperwork. She had walked enough to get her municipal mutation done. She was now tackling the mutation for her land tax. She wanted her Subhashgram property papers in order. 'I'm a cow whose shed has burnt once,' she says, referring to the fiasco with her village land.

On her tout's advice, she had taken a day off to visit the land tax office, deep in the southern suburbs of Calcutta. She carried with her photocopies of her property deed as well as the seller's, and receipts of the land tax that she'd been paying in the seller's name. Based on these documents, the office was to process the mutation and issue her a tax receipt in her name. When she reached the office at 10 a.m., the line was already long; her turn came at 1.30 p.m. She submitted her documents and was told that the receipt— not the tax receipt, but receipt for these documents—would be issued at 4 p.m. 'That was around the time when Ma was very close to the end. While waiting for my receipt, I got a frantic call from Didi: come quick, she doesn't look good!' Buttermilk couldn't wait for her receipt. She found a Subhashgram neighbour who was willing to pick it up and hand it to the designated clerk. She then rushed off to see Bashona.

What happened next is unclear. But when Buttermilk went back to the tax office—another day off work—the clerk looked over her file and said: everything is in order, but where's the receipt? 'When

I heard this my stomach sank,' she said, her face clenched. 'Did my neighbour not give the receipt to the clerk? Or is the clerk lying? Who knows? Will I have to do all of this over again? I would, but I've returned the seller's deed after making a copy. It had many pages and cost me 125 rupees! I didn't make two. All this money, effort, days off work, waiting in line for hours—and now this?'

Her story left me winded. I tried to imagine navigating the corridors of a mystifying state, blindfolded, led by murky agents, being chewed up and spat out of the maze, only to have to re-enter it. I would've been crushed and given up. Buttermilk doesn't. She deploys an astute mix of wile and empathy to plot out a fresh path.

'You know what I think?' Her face relaxes as a plan begins to congeal. 'I think my tout has a copy of the seller's deed. And don't I know these clerks? I'm sure he has the receipt. He's thinking, let me push her around a bit, I'll get some more money. That's fine. I'll walk some more. You guys eat your grass. Just get my job done.' Then she adds: 'Here's the thing: god has left me blind. I can't read or write, so I have to depend on others. And if you depend, you're going to get swindled. Otherwise, am I less than anyone?'

Indeed, in a year or so she had completed her land tax mutation.


The most desirable perk in the pre-election bonanza is the voter card. In the run-up to elections, handlers from political parties arrange voter-card camps in urban and suburban neighbourhoods, and in villages. The stated goal is worthy: get as many new voters to exercise their franchise as possible. But everyone knows that a voter card has little to do with voting—it is a valuable photo ID and address proof without which the poor are denied state benefits. So, if a party helps you get one you vote for them. At least the first time.

What Buttermilk dearly wanted, much more than free mutton curry and ice-cream, was a voter card at her Subhashgram address. Without it she couldn't prove she lived there. She couldn't open a bank account at Subhashgram, nor acquire a range of government IDs. She already had a voter card, but at her village address. She could get the address changed, with a lot of walking. But she didn't want to. She worried that giving up her village voter card would further undermine her already fraught landownership there. The only option was illicit: a second voter card. And the promiscuous pre-election air gave her hope.

She had even lined up a tout, but luck failed her. Before she could get very far in her voter card quest she got hit by the Aadhaar card tsunami.


Aadhaar is a biometric-based identity card originally intended to plug leaks in the public distribution system serving India's poor. The state planned to collect biometric data—fingerprints and iris scans—of over a billion Indians, to be stored in a central database, linked to name, address and banking details. The data would be used to verify the identity of a subsidy recipient and directly deposit the subsidy, thereby eliminating predatory middlemen. When the government floated Aadhaar in 2010 and tried to make it mandatory for state subsidies, it met with stiff resistance from opposition lawmakers in parliament. The concerns were many: lack of adequate infrastructure for a technology-driven public distribution system, the vast data trove being vulnerable to theft, and its collection violating privacy. The state continued to gather biometric profiles by executive fiat. This led to lawsuits.

The Supreme Court of India ruled—twice, in 2013 and in 2015—

that Aadhaar could not be made mandatory for state subsidies. The Union government changed hands in between, in mid-2014. The new party in power had vociferously argued against Aadhaar when in opposition but now championed it. The data gathering by fiat continued unabated. Moreover, the new government expanded Aadhaar's ambit to cover a plethora of domains not in the original initiative, sufficiently altering its nature that it began to resemble, for many, a state surveillance tool.

In order to codify Aadhaar into law, the bill would need pass both houses of parliament. The ruling party had an absolute majority in the lower house but not in the upper. Given the level of concern about the Aadhaar initiative, there was a good chance such a bill would fail. In March 2016, the government skirted this obstacle by bundling the Aadhaar Act with the annual Money Bill that only needs to pass in the lower house. Aadhaar had become law by weaselling through a loophole, even as it was being actively fought in the courts.

As the Union government had aggressively pushed Aadhaar while the courts insisted it was voluntary, enrolment had been uneven nationwide. Some states had embraced it, others had resisted. Bengal was in the latter camp. But now, with the forced passage of the Aadhaar Act, the poor stood to lose their subsidies— LPG, kerosene, grain—unless they acquired their Aadhaar card in short order. On the eve of its own re-election bid, this threw the Bengal government into a tizzy. It scrambled to set up Aadhaar enrolment camps all over the state. Away from the cities, these camps were few and far between, many in makeshift structures, manned by untrained operators mopped up in the frenzy.

Because her voter card was at her village address, Buttermilk needed to travel there to enrol for her Aadhaar card. The entire family went together: Buttermilk, Jhoro, Bonomali, Rupa. Three out of the four needed to take the day off work. Their designated camp, in a Panchayat office, was catering to seven villages. They joined the snaking queue at 10 a.m. By midday, over 500 people were waiting in line, in brain-curdling heat. There was no shade. And no toilets. 'We were all wilting,' Buttermilk said. 'They were letting the old folks go ahead. But think of the women carrying little kids they couldn't leave behind. Can you stand like that for long? They sat on the dirt path.' Hours went by as the line inched forward. No one knew how long this was going to take. Snack vendors had gathered and were having a field day. 'Around 2 o'clock, we had to eat something. I went to a mooriwallah to get my throat cut. You won't believe how much he was asking for two scoops: ten rupees! I told him to add extra green chillies. I figured the hot chillies would force us to drink more water, so we'd need less moori to feel full!' A striking life hack. 'My husband and son were soon hissing and sweating like steam engines. I had to go find more water for them.'

The sun became old and lenient, then twilight faded to darkness. It was 8 p.m. by the time their turn came. The operator was to fill a form based on the information in the voter card and take biometric scans. Jhoro, Bonomali and Rupa got theirs done without a hitch. For Buttermilk, the fingerprint scanner baulked. 'Not all my fingertips were showing up. So, shouldn't you be patient? I had waited in line for ten hours! No, he was asking me to leave, because there were so many still waiting. I couldn't take it anymore. I broke down in tears,' her voice cracked. 'Seeing that he softened and said: Ma, what's wrong? I said: the LPG account is in my name, and it's mine that didn't work?' She would be denied her LPG subsidy without an Aadhaar card. The operator, perhaps at the end of his tether, suggested that Buttermilk change the LPG account to her husband's name—another crippling time sink. He then pushed her out with a final bit of advice: 'We'll hold another camp next month. Apply cream on your hands meanwhile to soften them.' Recounting this, Buttermilk looked at her hands and chuckled. The ridiculous had bubbled through the carapace of tragedy.

Buttermilk's fingertips are callused from decades of swabbing floors and doing laundry. This is true of an overwhelming majority of Indians because their hands are used in manual labour. The designers of the Aadhaar project had incorporated the iris scan for this reason, realising that a system based on fingerprints alone was unlikely to work. The system, as designed, allows the applicant to submit only her iris scan. Moreover, not all ten fingerprints need to successfully scan. The applicant is to be notified which fingers had failed so she doesn't use them when being verified. But of course, Buttermilk knew none of this. Neither, it appeared, did the operator.

In the tearing rush to collect 1.3 billion biometric profiles—a task outsourced to private operators of questionable training—the quality of the data was a casualty. This would bring inordinate grief to the most vulnerable Indians: the rural poor who rely on government food subsidies, the children who rely on their school lunches, the students who rely on their government scholarships. Even with a valid Aadhaar card, many would be denied benefits because the verification scan of their fingertips failed to match those in the database. Often verification was impossible in rural areas simply because the scanner failed to talk to the central server due to lack of connectivity, or power. One could view this as teething troubles, as a good idea botched by hasty and sloppy implementation. But the horizon where the wrinkles were worked out seemed far. And the ensuing grief was pervasive and real.

Buttermilk felt the grief. But she didn't take her failures personally. Her focus was on how to restore her LPG subsidy without missing too many days of work. She didn't care whose fault it was, who broke the system or why. For her, it was quite simply about the money: about 2,000 rupees a year.

With more walking and sheer doggedness, she eventually did get her Aadhaar card. But that was not enough. She submitted a copy of it to her LPG supplier. She now needed to supply her bank—in the village—with her Aadhaar details so that her LPG subsidy would be directly deposited into her account. This was another one of those wait-in-line-all-day affairs. And when her turn came, she was told she didn't have all the documents, she'd have to come back. At this point I had to ask her why she wasn't angry. 'Who should I be angry with?' she said with great calm. 'My neighbours didn't give me good information. I found out later that everyone else in line had all their documents. I didn't have the time, so I'd told Rupa to ask around our neighbourhood and find out. And this is what she came back with. So, I yelled at her!' She yells at Rupa, but not at the state.

Buttermilk is never exercised about the Indian state. She seems to view it as some form of feral life, addled and unpredictable, which fortunately stays largely out of sight. Because when it does appear, it might attack. And who in their right mind gets angry at marauding wildlife? The notions of rights and justice are foggy, and not worth the time. The smart thing to do is to watch, prepare and get out of the way. Like you would for a mad tusker on the loose. The really smart thing, though, is to somehow marshal that tusker to rampage through the grove you wanted flattened anyway.

After her Aadhaar fever had subsided, Buttermilk came to work one day with glad tidings: 'They are giving us new toilets!' In a furious push to eradicate public defecation nationwide, the government was going to build a toilet in every home that didn't have one, in exchange for 900 rupees—a heavily subsidised sum. Enforcing their usage, of course, was outside the purview of this project.

'But don't you already have a toilet?' I had used it on visits to her Subhashgram home.

'Ahhaa, that was given in CPM's time,' she clucked at my naiveté. 'Now Trinamool is giving, why shouldn't we take?' This was a Union government scheme disbursed by the states and Trinamool was the ruling party in Bengal. 'If another party comes later, and they hand out toilets, we'll take theirs too!'

But she was far from a mindless toilet collector. Buttermilk had a plan. 'They came and built the toilet but I didn't let them finish the work!' she said conspiratorially. The work, as intended, was to dig a well to install a sewage tank, connect a sewer line to the toilet bowl set into a cement floor, and build a room around it, complete with a fibreglass roof and a door. Buttermilk had set aside a spot in her yard for this installation. 'When the crew arrived, I told them: don't worry about the bottom' – that is, the business end of the loo – 'just make sure the room is nicely done.' The lead mason baulked at this. 'He said: "Aunty, if they find out at the party office, they'll take away my day's wage!" I said: "No no, I'd never mention your name! I'll say they came in a hurry, I wasn't ready, so they dug in the wrong spot. Arrey, I'll build a toilet, don't worry. I'll just move it a bit.'" She didn't let the crew put in the toilet bowl.

'You see, the room that they're giving us,' she explained, 'is twice as big as what you need for a loo. So, here's my plan: use half of it for a bath and the other half for a loo. The CPM loo I'll keep, that's more solid work. What they're doing this time is low quality. And my current bath?' A luminous smile now. 'That's going to become my kitchen!' A corner of her covered porch is where she cooks now.

Buttermilk came up to my desk one morning. 'Here,' she said, her eyes sparkling, and handed me a laminated photo ID. It was a voter card in her name at her Subhashgram address.

'This is truly impressive! How did you pull this off?' I knew how much she had wanted this.

'A good tout,' she grinned. 'And 200 rupees.'

'How long did it take?'

'About six months.' I knew someone who had moved her Delhi voter card to Bombay on the legitimate route. It had taken ten years. 'The tout said he can even move my Aadhaar card to Subhashgram. But that'll be more pricey.'

Besides, she had just straightened out the Aadhaar linkage with her bank and was finally receiving her LPG subsidies. She wasn't about to rock that boat right away. 'What I want now is a bank account at Subhashgram.' She looked like what I imagine mountaineers in the 8,000-metres club look like as they scratch off each peak from their list. 'But they need two forms of ID at that address. So I went ahead and got my PAN card as well.'

'Why would you need a PAN card? You're not a taxpayer,' I pointed out.

'Of course I pay taxes'—Buttermilk was indignant—'land tax, property tax.'

'That's different. PAN is for income tax.'

'Oh.' A brief pause. I could tell she didn't know what income tax was. 'Anyway. It's best to get it done. Are you seeing this government's moves? Who knows what they'll ask for next!'

Her tout was working on getting her bank account done, which she had decided was going to be jointly held with Jhoro. 'Because I'm going to start walking for his unemployment card. He needs a bank account for that. His health is broken, he can barely work anymore. If the benefits at least cover his smokes, that'd be a relief.'

She was going to keep walking. There were more peaks to climb.

# 11

# A Sense of Place

Subhashgram, a low-income suburb about 25 kilometres south of Calcutta, rose on what once were rice fields adjoining a clutch of villages. One of these—Kodalia—is Subhas Chandra Bose's ancestral village. Buttermilk knows him. 'Netaji Subhas Bose. He freed the country,' she says with utter lack of conviction, a child reciting rote. Her view of India's Independence Day, though, is rather more firm.

'Of course I know about that,' she retorts. 'It's a festival! It happens every year at the end of Sraabon.' Sraabon is the Bengali calendar month that ends mid-August.

'A festival?'

'Yes. A festival for the educated. They get a holiday and have fun.'

'Who do you mean?'

'Arrey, it's them, those who go to schools and colleges. In the morning that day they do a pujo in front of a flag. Then there's music and biriyani. I've seen it!'

'But you don't get the day off?'

She finds the suggestion absurd and has a laughing fit. 'I don't,' she says, wiping away laugh tears, 'neither do factory workers.'

'But it is a national holiday!'

'Every factory stays open. You can go check. But those who grind pens in offices, they get a break.'

We were chatting while walking down Subhashgram's main thoroughfare, a road named after Subhas Bose's father Janaki Nath Bose, and not his more famous son. Kodalia is an old place. Its fame long predates Subhas Bose.

As early as the mid-nineteenth century, Kodalia and its neighbouring villages—Arbeliya, Changripota, Maloncho—formed an unusual locus of thought and energy. Dwarakanath Bidyabhushan (1819–1886), a Sanskritist and social reformer, set up a printing press in his Changripota home in 1862 to publish *Somprokash*, a journal geared towards raising social and political awareness. Tarakumar Kobiratno (1843–1935) of Arbeliya, was a poet and editor of the *Bamabodhini Potrika*, a late nineteenth-century journal championing women's rights. Satkori Bandopadhyay (1889–1935) of Maloncho was a renowned anti-British revolutionary who was arrested in 1930 and died in jail. M.N. Roy (1887–1964) of Kodalia founded the Mexican Communist Party in 1917, and in 1920, commissioned by Lenin, founded the Communist Party of India at Tashkent. There were many others, a constellation that Subhas Chandra Bose would later join.

Kodalia continued to be a hub of literary and political activity into the 1940s, when Salil Chowdhury, then a local youth who went on to be a renowned musician and composer, organised a peasant movement here along with his colleagues from the Indian People's

Theatre Association. Chowdhury's first mass song, *Desh Bhesechey Baaner Joley,* was composed in 1942 protesting administrative apathy towards floods here that would maul the surrounding rice crop each year.

Those floods have a lot to do with why Buttermilk lives in Subhashgram.


The Kodalia cluster once stood on the banks of the Adi Ganga river, the original channel of the Ganga as it meets the Bay of Bengal. The surrounding land, nourished and drained by the river, was top-grade. The famed sons of Kodalia were also sons of wealthy landowning families, the wealth a direct result of the river's largesse. That river is now dead.

This didn't happen overnight. In the late seventeenth century, a canal was built—evidence suggests, by the Dutch—to divert water westwards into the Hooghly for the ease of ocean-bound trade armadas. Over time, this made the Hooghly the main channel and caused the Adi Ganga to lose flow. In the 1770s, William Tolly of the British East India Company built a canal to revive it, staving off the inevitable. But lack of regular de-silting slowly choked Tolly's canal and the Adi Ganga continued to recede. By the 1930s it could no longer drain its hinterland, which began to see devastating floods every monsoon. The river stayed somewhat navigable until the late 1970s. But by the 1990s, a building boom driving Calcutta's southern sprawl had reduced it to a rope of putrid sludge. An elevated metro track, with pillars driven directly into the river's bed, was the final nail in its coffin. A river was dead and a flood-prone Kodalia was en route to becoming Subhashgram.

As the floods continued to worsen, the landholding families

cut their losses by sectioning their rice paddies into lots and selling them off. The prices were low enough to be affordable for the urban poor wanting to upgrade from slum life. Buttermilk bought her 1,500-square-feet lot in 1999 for 18,000 rupees.

I had heard that Subhas Bose's family homestead still stands. When I asked Buttermilk how one gets there, she said she would find out. Buttermilk knew that Subhashgram was named after Subhas Bose, but then a lot of things are—parks, lakes, roads, even an international airport. That an abstraction like Bose could have physical traces in her own neighbourhood was a different matter entirely. She came back thrilled: 'I've lived here all these years and I had no idea! Now I'm asking around and everyone seems to have seen it. Even my husband has been. How come I haven't?' She had already formed a plan: 'You'll come, have a bit of lunch, rest, and then we'll go see it together. I have directions.'

The 'bit of lunch' turned out to be a veritable feast: rice, lentils, fried brinjals, pnui greens with pumpkins, carp stewed with tomatoes, catfish in a ginger-garlic braise. Rupa had cooked it all on Buttermilk's command, hunched over the stove in one corner of their covered porch. 'I don't get to show off her skills often, you see,' Buttermilk said, putting a benign spin on the nature of her commission. 'Have some more. The brinjals, pnui and pumpkin are all from my patch!' Bonomali, Buttermilk and I sat eating on the floor of one of their two rooms; Jhoro sat on the porch, next to the kitchen. Rupa served us all before serving herself, also on the porch. As they ate, she and Jhoro chatted in a low voice, with the occasional titter. Underlings in Buttermilk's regime, they clearly shared a special bond.

Buttermilk showed me around her yard after lunch. It felt spacious. About half the lot was built up: two rooms connected by a covered porch, raised enough to need a three-step stoop that was smooth and inviting. At the bottom of the yard, a coconut palm towered above an outhouse and bath. Its roots were exposed. The area being flood-prone, Buttermilk had to pour several truckloads of earth to elevate the lot before building. And she had scavenged sackfuls of rubble from the city to further raise the foundation of her home. The coconut palm was at the boundary with an unbuilt lot—nearly four feet lower, a swamp teeming with reeds. Any soil covering the palm's roots washed away into the swamp. 'This is how high the water is in my yard, every monsoon,' Buttermilk said, pointing at a watermark on her boundary wall, about two feet off the ground. The water laps at the second step of her stoop, so her rooms manage to stay dry. The dead river was going to haunt her forever.

But life finds a way. Bonomali shimmied up the palm with simian ease and twisted off a green coconut for me, its water sweet and refreshing. A grove of bananas, heavy with fruit, nestled the coconut palm. Next to the grove was a busy vegetable patch: brinjals, tomatoes, chillies, radishes, and all manner of Bengal's greens—pnui, kolmi, notey. A pumpkin vine snaked up the porch grille all the way to the asbestos roof where it laid hefty dividends. During those in-between stretches when the village land does its own thing, Jhoro works this little yard like a maniac. His wizard green thumb had left prints everywhere.

I noticed a striking hibiscus, as big as a baby's head, with spectacular red and white stripes.

'Won't you pick that?' I asked.

'No,' Buttermilk was firm, 'that stays on the bush.'

'Where?' the autowallah asked, his face scrunched, unsure of what he had heard.

'Gardeskul,' Buttermilk repeated, slower this time. 'Gard-es-kul.'

'What skul?' A penny dropped. 'Aaah, you mean girls' school! Why didn't you just say so?'

Buttermilk wasn't about to let an autowallah upstage her in public. 'I don't know about all that,' she said in a huff, 'I'm just repeating what I was told.'

Her move backfired. The autowallah now had an opening to lecture her: 'So just say it in Bengali—meyeder iskul—finished!'

Buttermilk looked gutted, her face a mottled bruise. Her illiteracy had spilt out in the open, like wet innards. I've often wondered what she's thinking at times like this, caught as she is between her quality and her station.

We were taking an auto to Subhas Bose's homestead, using the directions Buttermilk had gathered, evidently with some lossy bits. She was quiet for the ten-minute ride. But by the end of it, she had gotten her mojo back. When we got off and I started to pay the fare, she shot me a glance. There was a quiet heft in it that said: your money is no good here. I was her guest.

The girls' school where we got off was founded by Subhas Bose's father, J.N. Bose, in 1916. It still wore a bit of festive regalia from its centenary celebrations. We walked down the road named after J.N. Bose towards the home he once lived in.

It turned out there wasn't much to see. The Bose family homestead, like many of its ilk, is a decrepit mansion bearing indifferent signage and a bilious caretaker. The vast grounds have become partially encroached so that the various buildings in the compound no longer seem to be part of anything whole. The library stood out. Still very much in use by the locals, it glowed like a well-thumbed volume in a dusty archive. J.N. Bose had founded this library in 1920 in the memory of his father, Haranath Bose. The library has a raised and covered porch that makes a natural performance space, with an adjoining field for the audience to gather in. It was here, in the early 1940s, that local artists had performed Jyotirindra Moitra's rousing songs from *Nabajibaner Gaan*—on the Bengal famine—to a huge crowd. And it was here that Bijon Bhattacharya's powerful one-act play *Jobanbondi* (Confession) had been performed. This was hallowed ground.

Buttermilk was delighted that her guest was thrilled. 'I live in such a place and I didn't have a clue!' she marvelled. 'Now that I've seen it, I don't need to ask anyone for directions. Babbah!' She had exorcised the incident with the autowallah.

Next to the library was a splendid yellow-ochre gateway, double-pillared on either side with an ornamental peaked lintel. This was once the main entrance to the Bose family compound. A marble plaque on it read 'Haranath Lodge'. It stood forlorn, a gate to nowhere. The ageing light had burnished it gold. Buttermilk stood framed by this gateway bearing Subhas Bose's grandfather's name, looking like a droplet that had found its nook.


On our way back, she mentioned another ruin. 'This one I've seen before. Its bones are all showing. And it's always dark because of huge trees. Looks haunted.' She took me there, a short walk away. It was indeed a mansion, enormous and in a state of photogenic ruination, mature banyans both helpfully scaffolding and destroying it. It was set back from the road, deep within the gloom of a vast tree-filled compound. There was a pond that Buttermilk remembered being much larger. 'They're filling it up,' she said. The compound was shabbily fenced with corrugated tin. Truckloads of stone chips and sand had been dumped nearby. This property was amidst shifting shape.

Kodalia was once home to many mansions. Whose could this one have been? I spotted two elderly men sitting at a nearby teashop. Maybe they would know. 'Oh, that one?' one of them drawled through ill-fitting dentures. 'That was M.N. Roy's home.' There was no signage.

The house in Mexico City that M.N. Roy lived in around the time of founding the Communist Party of Mexico in 1917 still bears his name, however. That it is now an exclusive night club is another matter.

# 12

# Folidol '15

Buttermilk's debts were piling up. She had borrowed heavily for her daughters' weddings. She had borrowed to upgrade her Subhashgram home from mud to brick. And more recently, she had borrowed to fix the mud floor in her village home because an army of rats had burrowed through it into her rice silo. When I tried to talk her into living within her means, risk-averse Bengali that I am, she told me about the elderly matriarch of a Marwari home she works in—her debt philosopher and chief creditor rolled into one. 'My Subhashgram home would get damaged every monsoon when it was mud-thatch. Every year I would run to Ma and say, give me some money, I need repairs. One year she sat me down and said, listen, beti, you're pouring this money down the drain. Why don't you put up a brick-mortar home instead, that'd be permanent. I said, where am I going to get the money? She said, arrey, you'll borrow! Even we have to borrow, otherwise our business gets stuck. When you're in debt, there is fear in your heart, it puts fire in your work. Borrow, work hard and pay it off. Don't get stuck. I've followed her advice since then. I'm no longer afraid.'

In spite of such sage advice from the temple of Mammon, Buttermilk continued to fail to find its gates. Matters came to a head in April 2015 over her boro harvest, the same crop whose planting I had witnessed at her village a few months before.


Mid-April is Poila Boishakh, the Bengali new year. This is an auspicious time in rural Bengal, with morphed urban residues. The last day of the year, Choitro Shonkranti, is one of public festivities and scenes of graphic theatre, of men pierced with hooks spinning centrifugally on poles. Away from this effusion, there are quiet rituals in every rural home.

'I've just sent my husband to the village,' Buttermilk said. 'Poila Boishakh is day after tomorrow. The paddies are nearly ready for harvest. There are several things to do in the village now. One in particular my mother-in-law can't do. And I have to work. So he has to go.'

'What is it?'

'Before the first sunrise of the year, everyone has to light a fire on their land.'

'What sort of fire?' I couldn't picture ripe paddies burning.

'We make torches out of twisted straw with a bamboo handle, light them up and stick them into one corner of the paddy. One in every parcel. If we don't, someone else might. Then he gets a claim on that parcel—he's lit it, you see. The land expects to be lit. Our home's courtyard is also similarly lit. This work my husband does, otherwise I would have to rush.'

It was a vivid visual: every parcel of farmed land in rural Bengal lit with torches, before the first rays of the year touch the heaving grain. Because the land expects it, she said. Buttermilk had left me with this in the morning. The same afternoon, a freakish storm presented a different register of vividness.

Afternoon storms this time of year are a Bengali thing; we even have a word for it: kalboishakhi, the dark one of Boishakh. Dark both in colour and in menace. The script is simple. April brings searing heat; the hot air rises, brings in cooler air and sucks moisture from the Bay. By afternoon, tall columns of thunderhead clouds gather. A lick of cool breeze is your cue for battening windows. Because within minutes a fierce wind will kick up a whirlwind of dust, whip lanky trees into Cs, and muss up canopies like so many reeds. It may rip off a piece of fibreglass and slice something with it. Once the storm is spent, a welcome rain clears and cools the air. The whole thing is over in less than an hour.

What happened that afternoon was not just any kalboishakhi. The laden sky took on a fearsome jaundiced hue. A vicious wind groaned like a feral beast trapped. The storm lasted nearly two hours. It felled trees and damaged homes throughout the city. But what I remember is the blizzard. A towering silk cotton tree nearby had already popped its seedpods, this being the season. The storm huffed out the tree's load, like a giant dandelion, and a million cotton fluffs took flight. They swirled about in the pallid light against a muscular sky. A lost blizzard in the wrong hemisphere on a hot day.


Buttermilk's storm was different. She came to work the next day, her face ashen. 'I was on my train home when the storm hit,' she said. 'The wind came up like a giant whistling iron, pressing everything flat! I huddled at Subhashgram station until things calmed down. On my walk home, I kept seeing fallen homes. One's asbestos roof was ripped off, another's wall was damaged. Nearly a dozen! I began to shudder. Was mine still standing? Luckily, it is. Babbah! But Rupa was scared witless. She said, it felt like a hundred roaring bulls were charging her at full tilt! I can't tell you how many trees are down, some of them huge.' She took a breath. 'But the real story is in the village. It's all finished,' she said, her voice cracking. 'Only two weeks from harvest. All heavy with milk. You saw it at planting. I can't tell you how beautifully the rice was coming up this time. Like a green cloud. This high'— she held a hand level with her mid-thigh—'as far as the eye goes! My husband says they're all lying flattened, like an elephant has mauled them.' She wiped her tears and collected herself. 'Those plants that have snapped, their grains won't harden. Those that are simply bent, theirs will. But you can't tell which is which before threshing. So we have to spend the money to harvest it all. At threshing, the hardened paddy will fall to the floor and the empty ones will fly. Only then will we know how much paddy gives how much rice.' This Bengali idiom—meaning, to know what's what— she deftly deployed here both literally and metaphorically.

Buttermilk had taken on additional debt for this crop. Because it was shaping up to be a bumper yield, she had hoped to recoup her investment and perhaps even keep a bit of profit. Ten days after this catastrophe, her damaged crop was further hit by a furious rain storm. The flattened rice plants, some snapped, some bent, had been left on the fields to dry out before harvesting. They were all inundated now. In the parcel she called her ditch, the water was thigh-high. The paddy, whatever had survived, was at risk of rotting. And the skies hadn't yet let up.

Buttermilk came to work a few days later, gaunt, her eyes in a thousand-yard stare. I saw her doing the floors with uncharacteristic listlessness. I was preoccupied with a fifth-century Javanese rock inscription when she came up to my desk.

'What's that medicine on the window sill of the laundry bathroom? The one in the small aluminium canister.' Her voice was hoarse.

'I'm not sure,' I said distractedly. 'If you bring it over I might be able to tell you.'

She brought it over. The label had a picture of plants and said: Metacid 50, contact insecticide. I told her it was a type of poison, to kill insects. 'Yes, it's poison,' she said heatedly. 'Why do you keep such poison at home?' There was a strange glint in her eyes.

I hadn't the foggiest idea. Her tone got me defensive. I reached back and remembered that I had once gotten enthused about ridding a beloved street dog of mange. Perhaps it was a leftover from that project? I didn't know and I was a bit miffed. I wanted to get back to work.

'Why are you so excited about this all of a sudden?'

'I know this poison.' She looked like she was in a trance. 'It's Folidol. Don't keep it at home.' She had a wan smile, but her eyes were on fire. 'My head is in a whirl. I might do something. Please, please remove it.'

Folidol. That old friend of erased farmers. I finally grasped what she was saying. Stunned, I got off my desk to comfort her. At my touch, she slumped to the floor, wracked with sobs. I sat with her and tried to scrape up soothing words, all the while quaking within. I felt the metallic taste of fear in my mouth, the fear of losing her. Its force surprised me. But I wasn't going to share any of this with her. Instead, I kept up a patter of inanities: that she was a battle-hardened tank, it wasn't like her to run away, what about the weaklings she would leave behind? She calmed down after a bit and told me what had brought this on.

The crop loss had stung her deep. But she was coping with it when the news came that a twenty-seven-year-old farmer in her village, his crop similarly destroyed, had killed himself drinking Folidol. This was someone Buttermilk had known since he was a toddler. That image was hounding her. 'If the kid could do this …' she trailed off, tears welling up again. I tried coming up with ways in which she was different from the young farmer. But she wasn't listening. 'I can't trust myself,' she said urgently. 'Please remove the poison. I've removed all the kerosene from my Subhashgram home.' Jhoro and Bonomali were away at the village picking up the pieces. And Rupa was there too, on kitchen duty. Buttermilk was spending the nights alone in Subhashgram, marinating in suicidal thoughts.

But this storm, too, Buttermilk weathered. She came to work a few days later, fresh-faced and utterly serene, the vermillion on her parting just so. Was this the preternatural calm of one whose back had hit the wall?

'It rained three hours straight yesterday,' she said, with a sweet smile, looking up from sweeping.

'Wait, you mean at the village?' I sputtered.

'Yes, but I'm not thinking about it,' she said, airily waving her free hand. 'What's gone is gone!'

'Have you started pumping the water out?'

'No, where? Our whole village shares one pump. Everyone's

fields are flooded. And the sky still looks like an old blanket. What's the point of pumping out water when you know more is on the way?'

'But isn't the grain going to rot?'

'My husband went into the paddies. He thinks only some of the plants have snapped. If there's a good dry stretch we may still get a partial harvest. But only the one dozing up in that old blanket knows.'

Then a little later: 'I'm cracking my head over this harvest, but let me tell you about the real crackpots in my life. Rupa hates it, but I've sent her to the village to help out my mother-in-law. The men are all there now for the harvest, it's a lot of work in the kitchen. So she calls me yesterday, "O Ma, Ma, I've burnt my hand!" She was making loochi, while rolling out the dough she found a bug in it, plucked it out and threw it away, but it happened to land in the hot oil, which splattered and now she has blisters.

'I said: "So, will we need to amputate the hand?"

'"No, no," she said.

'"That's good. Which hand?"

'"The left."

'"So you still have the right, you can make do."

'"But Ma, the blisters are full of water!"

'"So's our land. Once the land dries, your blisters will dry too."' Buttermilk delivered this deadpan, then burst out laughing.

She had bounced back, like a human hit-me doll.


The land did get a good sunny stretch in early May. Things dried out somewhat. Buttermilk's three-bigha ditch still had waist-deep water, but her one bigha had been harvested. The wet sheaves of paddy were laid out on the glutinous mud. The hope was to dry the grain before rot set in. Some of it had germinated. A bad sign.

'On a usual harvest, that one bigha meets my family's rice needs for a whole year,' Buttermilk said. 'But who knows what we'll get this time. Also, this is the skinny grain. I've told you, we don't like eating it because it doesn't stick. We plant it to sell. To city people like you. But this time, we won't be able to. We'll have to eat it.'

'But why won't you be able to sell? Everyone's harvest has been hit. Won't the prices go up?'

'If flat-people like you take a look at this grain, you won't want to buy it. It's yellowed, with brown splotches. Some will crumble when handled. It won't sell.'

In mid-May, Buttermilk heard the news she had been waiting for: her one bigha had yielded eleven sacks of paddy after threshing, about half the usual. 'I'll have to take the next two days off,' she said. 'They've dumped the sacks on the courtyard, it's all wet!' Eleven sacks of paddy, 55 kilos each. 'I'm going to go spread the grain out, dry it and then gather it up in the silo. They won't be able to do this right. I'm catching a train this afternoon, I'll work the next two days straight—like a maniac—then catch a dawn train back to city work.' She laid out this gruelling schedule with the glee of a vacation plan. She still wasn't sure how much rice this paddy would yield after husking. 'But at least I got something!' she cried, awash in relief. With all her land eventually harvested, she felt there would be at least enough rice to feed her family for the year.

But she had taken heavy losses on this crop, nearly a quarter of her annual income. There was no time to whinge about that. It was time to borrow more; there were payments to be made. 'The invitations have arrived,' Buttermilk said. Like all things old and worn, even payment in farm work has its own aesthetics. The day-labourers get paid daily, but the others providing services to the farmer—spreading fertiliser, spraying pesticide, driving the tractor or the mobile-pump unit—wait until the harvest is in the silo. At that point, they send the farmer a formal invitation. 'It's like a wedding card, all red and yellow.' The farmer is expected to come and enjoy a light snack and settle the accounts before leaving. This harvest was hobbled, but the invitations still had to be serviced. And Buttermilk was already looking ahead to the next season, to another round of Russian roulette.

'Now that the boro crop is out, the tractors will come and give the earth a turn. Then we let it sit. The hard heat of May cures it. There's usually a good shower or two around the end of May. That brings up a sea of grass, which soon dries to a crisp. With the first monsoon rains in mid-June, this dried grass rots into the best fertiliser. In that juicy, well-fed soil, the seeds go in. And as the rains really open up in July, we break the seedbeds, replant, and the amon rice comes up like a green flood!' The imagined verdure brought on a radiant smile. 'At least that's how it's supposed to be. But if you don't get the right water at the right time? Death. It's all in god's hands.' The land's fine-tuned rice calendar is fragile. Buttermilk hasn't heard of climate change but she can feel it. 'We got flooded to death this boro harvest. Maybe we'll be dried to death during the next amon planting. Who knows?'


As her harvest fever receded, I ventured to extract a promise from Buttermilk. 'Don't worry,' she said sheepishly, 'I won't consider suicide again.' This was coming mainly from a place of empathy. She seemed pained that the incident with the Folidol canister had rattled me. 'I know what suicide does to others,' she continued, her eyes welling up. 'I'm still carrying Baba's within me.' With that, the story of Karno's death breached whatever dam she was holding it in. It poured out of her in a cinematic torrent. She occasionally stopped to suck in air, hugging herself as if fresh scabs were being ripped off. But she kept going.

# 13

# Karno Parbo:
# Buttermilk's Telling

I've told you that Choto occupied our home in the Ponchanontola slum after Baba left for the village. A few years later, he decided to get the electricity bill transferred to his name. It was a natural thing to do. It's handy as address proof. But the thing that Choto did when filling out the form is instead of writing 'son of Karno Haldar', he wrote Ishwar—Late Karno Haldar. He had killed Baba on paper! It was probably an honest mistake. When Baba confronted Choto, he said, 'I'm sorry, I screwed up.' But Dada and Mejo were extremely riled up over this.

Baba told them, 'Choto admits it was a mistake. He's apologised and I accept.'

But they were having none of it: 'How can you forgive someone who calls you dead while you're alive?'

Baba fended them off and advised Choto, 'They may come provoke you. Be agreeable. Don't take their bait.'

Sometime after this incident, Mejo went to Choto one day and said, 'Give me the ration cards, I need to get some kerosene.'

Choto fetched the sleeve that had the whole family's ration cards, fished out Mejo's and gave it to him.

Mejo reacted, 'What's this? Why my card alone?'

'I'm the only one who's supporting our parents,' Choto said. 'I'm also looking after the sisters now that they're back in the slum.' This was 1996; Chutki and I were both back in the city, living in the slum and working homes. 'So, let everyone's cards stay with me. You keep yours.'

Mejo said, 'Let me see that sleeve.'

As soon as Choto handed it to him, he yanked out all the cards and ripped them to bits. You know how valuable ration cards are, and how hard to replace!

Choto was shocked: 'Why'd you do this? You could've said, okay, I'll support our parents, let the cards stay with me. Or, let's all look after them, and take turns with the cards. Why rip them up? Who does this hurt the most?'

Mejo smirked. 'We'll see who this hurts the most. The game has just begun!'

This happened around eleven in the morning. Mejo went straight from there to Baba's. As he arrived at the village, Baba was just sitting down to lunch with Thakuma. Ma was serving them rice. As Mejo walked in, Baba told Ma: 'O Bawro-bou, your Mejo-baba is here.' He glanced at Ma to ask: is there enough food? Ma gave him an assuring nod. But Baba still set aside half the rice on his plate and told Ma: 'After I finish, you take a bit more rice here and eat from my plate. Then there'll be enough for him.'

Mejo spoke up at this point. 'Ei, you son of a bitch'—he was speaking to Baba—'I haven't come to eat!' Baba looked up, not yet registering. Mejo went on: 'I'm not here to eat. I'm here to pick up all the dowry you took at my wedding. You think you're too big, eh? And your Choto-baba is your prince. I'll show you how much paddy gives how much rice!'

Baba could tell that Mejo was drunk. He knew all about drunkenness, so he was tender. 'Mejo-baba, you've come a long way. Sit and rest. Let me finish lunch. I'll look into this.'

Mejo railed, 'No, I want my dowry back now! Now! I want all the pots and pans and clothes and everything the bride's family gave you. And the 10,000 rupees you took from them!' This could never have been a sober request. It had been several years since Mejo's wedding.

'The stuff you haven't already taken is up in the attic,' Baba said. 'You can go pick them up. But where am I going to get the money? It was spent at your wedding. I can't give you the money.'

At this, Mejo flew off the handle and screamed: 'You can't give me the money? Or won't? You son of a whore!'

Thakuma was sitting right there, being called a whore.

Hearing this, Baba stood up and said, 'Let me go wash up.'

He was probably thinking he could calm Mejo down. But as soon he stood up, Mejo thought Baba was going to hit him. Ma and Thakuma thought the exact same thing. So they both wrapped their arms around Baba and held him back. With Baba restrained, Mejo picked up a heavy wooden club that was lying in the courtyard. These are used in the village for loosening the earth at the base of a tree. As the two women held Baba down, Mejo clubbed him hard on the side of his head. Yes, just like Karno in Mahabharot. My Baba was hit while pinned down.

He was bleeding. He kept trying to break free: 'Ma, Bawro-bou, let me go!' But they grabbed him even harder. Chutki was visiting

Baba at the time. She came rushing: 'Ei Mej-da, stop, why are you doing to this to Baba?' Hearing this, Mejo chased her with the club. Ma and Thakuma saw this as an opening and tried to drag Baba away from the courtyard, into the house. But Mejo came charging back and hit Baba again, on the other side of his head. This second blow knocked Baba out.

As he collapsed, Ma and Thakuma finally snapped back to their senses. They yelled at Mejo: 'What did you just do? Why? We were trying to take him away? Why did you hit him?'

Mejo was in a trance, he kept mumbling: 'I'm glad I did, I'm glad.' But his drink was wearing off. He was scared.

Meanwhile, Chutki had rushed over to my Kaka's house wildly screaming, 'Somebody help! Come right now! He's killing Baba!' They all came running and found Baba unconscious. In a bloody heap. My hardy Baba … wait, give me a minute …

They called a cycle-van and took him to the hospital. Then they informed us in Calcutta. I was at work. I didn't get the news until I got home in the evening. Choto and I conferred. He said, 'It's already late. Maybe we should go in the morning.'

I said, 'No, let's go. Trains run late on the Raydighi line.' He then reminded me that there was the risk of the baghrol to consider. You don't know about the baghrol? It's a type of monster that had appeared in the Sunderbans back then. It would prowl the night and maul people. I told Choto, 'I'm going no matter what.' So we went.

Dada had heard Baba's news earlier in the day but didn't budge. He and Mejo were always a team. After I came back to the slum and heard the news, I made a public promise: 'If something happens to Baba, I'm going after Mejo with everything I've got!' Dada heard this and said, 'Aaynh, she's like Surpanakha, landed here from the village to fight with us on Baba's behalf!' But he must have been rattled, because when he heard I was going to see Baba, Dada also left for the village. Mejo, meanwhile, had slinked away from the house and was waiting out at the Khanrapara crossing. The same Khanrapara crossing, where decades before I had waited hours for Baba to bring rice for the crab feast.

Choto and I went straight to the hospital in Raydighi. We saw Baba. He had needed six stitches on one side of his head and seven on the other. His head was swathed in a bandage. He was in pain, but stable. After we came out of the hospital, it was too late for any transport. From Raydighi we walked all the way to our village that night, over two hours. With the baghrol out and about! Dada was already there.

As I walked in, Thakuma and Ma got very agitated. 'What are you doing here? Your Dada's threatening to kill you!' They were quaking with fear. 'Did you say you're going to call the police, file a case, go after Mejo? He's saying he's going to kill you and stick you in the pond out back. Run, run away, right now!'

I said: 'No, why should I run? When I was coming from Calcutta, Choto reminded me of the baghrol. That didn't scare me off. Now, if Dada kills me and buries me in Baba's land, fine. I'm not moving.' I knew Dada was in the back room, within earshot. I said, 'But you know, Ma, if you dig a deep hole for someone else, there's always the danger that you might fall in yourself. Perhaps he's come for me, but who knows, maybe it'll be his body that floats up in the pond!' I wanted Dada to know that he can't mess with me. He didn't make a peep.

It had been a long day, so I slept hard. In the morning, I told Ma, once again within Dada's earshot: 'See? I'm not in the pond. I had a very restful night. Don't get spooked by empty threats. It is because you all got scared that this happened to Baba. If you had let him go, he wouldn't have hurt anyone. He would've maintained his calm and talked Mejo out of his frenzy. You pinned him down and gave Mejo the opening. He is a brainless lout and drunk on top of that. He couldn't tell whether he was beating up Baba or a street thug. You did this.'

Choto and I went back to the hospital to see Baba.

This time, he was speaking. He said, 'I won't show my face anymore.'

So we said, 'Why are you saying this? We're going to file a case.'

Then Baba told me, 'Listen to me, you're going to file a case alleging what? This is a matter between father and son. You won't be able to argue that the son has beaten up the father, because the father may have beaten up the son before! There is no case to be made here. Don't go to the police, Ma, I beg you. I'll go home, don't worry.'

'Then why did you say that you're not going to show your face?' I asked. 'Promise me, that you're not going to do anything funny when you get home.'

He promised us.

Baba stayed in the hospital for eighteen days. All those stitches had to dry. Then he went home and seemed to keep his promise. He seemed fine. He and Ma got back into their rhythm. A year went by.

Baba had been attacked in the winter of 1996. The following winter, he put up a large patch of French beans. They had just hit our markets back then and fetched a high price. His patch was shaping up to a bumper yield. Now, the pesticide vial that we found is not sold without a licence. Yes, Folidol. Baba had bought a large vial—250 grams—for his bean patch. This was early January, just before Mawkor Shonkranti. Baba's pattern was to wake up and drink toddy. He didn't used to drink much booze, but gallons of toddy. Toddy is how he filled up in the mornings.

That day he had his toddy and went to the big market at Raydighi. He bought a large fish and other groceries. Then he went to Ma's uncle's house in Raydighi town for a visit. They were delighted, he almost never went.

He came home and told Ma, 'Bawro-bou, I've got this large fish, do something special with it.' Ma set about cooking. When she was done, Baba asked whether she'd invited Thakuma.

Ma hadn't. So, Baba went over to my Kaka's house where my Thakuma was staying at the time, a few doors down.

He said, 'Ma, come have lunch with me today.'

Thakuma was a bit reluctant; she knew her sons could fly into a rage over nothing. She said, 'I'm not sure. These folks have already cooked for me.'

Baba then went to Kaka and said, 'I've got a large fish from Raydighi today and I wanted Ma to come have it with me. Will that be a problem?'

Kaka said, 'Of course not! Go right ahead.'

So, he brought Thakuma over, sat her down on the porch where they ate, and asked Ma to serve rice.

Ma said, 'But you haven't bathed yet.'

Baba said, 'I'll just go and come back in a flash. You set the places and begin serving.'

The women waited for him. And my two-year-old niece Noni toddled about. This was Chutki's girl, who Baba–Ma were looking after at the time while she worked in the city.

Baba came back from bathing. At some point when he went to take his bath, he had gone behind the house where he was soaking this other pesticide—it comes as white crystals, I don't remember the name. He went there and ate those crystals. This poison doesn't act right away. It slowly rots the gut. Before eating this, he'd only had toddy since the morning. He came back and sat down to lunch. Ma usually ate after him. But he insisted: 'No, today's different. Both of you, serve up. We're eating together today.' And Baba's word is law, so they began to eat. When they were about half done, Baba said: 'You two finish up. I'm not feeling too good. I'll go wash up.' He came back from washing up, went inside and lay down.

Ma didn't find any of this unusual. Baba often used to eat only part of his lunch because he was so full of toddy. He'd finish his food after napping off the buzz. But that day, before he lay down, Baba drained the entire vial of Folidol. Ma and Thakuma were eating on the porch, he was inside the room. They didn't notice anything. After drinking the Folidol, Baba pulled down the mosquito net over his cot and set the empty vial down on the floor. Now, Noni was Baba's pet, she loved to follow him everywhere. Baba realised that she might crawl over near his bed, find the vial and lick it, like she licks everything. So, he picked up the vial and chucked it on the roof of the net. Ma saw him chuck something and got alert. As Ma and Thakuma both got up and walked towards him, he was delirious: 'Ma, Ma, come here, see what I've done! Bawrobou, come near me. Noni, sweetie, come. Come!' They could smell the poison and saw the empty vial. They knew what he had done. Baba, ever sharp, had even thought of the possibility of Ma trying to drink some after she found out. He hadn't even left a drop in the vial for her.

Ma and Thakuma began to wail and everyone came running. Baba was in a strange state. He was jumping around, going indoors, coming out, pacing. It was as if a wild animal had sneaked into him. They called in a cycle-van to take him to the hospital. He refused to get on it. When they forced him, he smashed the van's wooden flatbed to pieces! He wanted to stay home. They called another cycle-van and this time tied him down to its bed with a rope. He strained against it. They set out for the hospital. After they'd been going for about ten minutes, he gradually became limp and fell silent. At the hospital, they washed his stomach. He puked volumes. He was also full of toddy, remember. The doctor said, since he's vomiting, since the bad water is leaving his system, he's going to pull through. But little did he know—none of us did— that Baba had popped those crystals beforehand.

He held on. Everyone thought he'll make it. The day he did this, Chutki and I got the news that evening after getting back from work. The earliest we could reach was the following evening. Me, Chutki, Choto and his wife. When we arrived, Baba spoke to us. He said, 'My lower back hurts.' He didn't say it like I just did. His speech was slurred. We couldn't make out what he was saying. After repeating it a few times, he pointed at his lower back. We finally understood and massaged it. Then we sat with him and talked to him for a bit. But it was getting late. So, we said: 'Baba, we'll leave now. Try and get some sleep. We'll be back in the morning.' Just as we were leaving the hospital, two of Baba's sisters were going in. They asked us how he was. We told them he seemed to be doing well, we just spoke with him. But we didn't know. Right after we left him, Baba had made his move. When my aunts arrived at his bedside, he was gone. Baba was gone. My Baba …

We didn't know any of this. Choto saw us women off at the Raydighi station and we caught the last train back to the city. He heard the news when he got back to the village. Death from poisoning is unnatural, so the hospital had to report it to the police. The police took several men from my family to the Raydighi police station for the night. I don't know all the details, but money changed hands. They called us in Calcutta early next morning with the news. They hadn't wanted us to cry all night.

Meanwhile, Baba was lying in the hospital morgue. Since this was a police case, there had to be a post-mortem. We waited and we waited. The night he died, the morgue doctor had been too swamped to get to Baba. When his shift changed the next morning, the new doctor refused to take Baba on. Baba had to spend that entire day in the morgue. Maybe out in the open, who knows. We finally got his body on the third day of his death.

Mejo had refused to come to the funeral. Kaka went and coaxed him to attend. He said, 'No one is pinning this on you. This is your last duty towards him.' Since Mejo's attack on Baba, we four sisters have had no real relationship with him or Dada. We talk, but there is no heart in it. Chutki won't even speak with Mejo. She had witnessed what he'd done to Baba.

We've all wondered why Mejo had wanted to pick a fight with Baba. Of us siblings, Mejo, Chutki and I have a bit of a peeled-nerve nature. We can get hot in the head and scary. Baba used the stick on all of us growing up, and later, we've all had verbal fights with him. But hitting Baba? That was unthinkable, even for Mejo, I'd say. He'd never done it before. He did have a special history with Baba, though. I don't know all of it. He grew up in the village, away from the rest of us, because that's what Baba had decided. When we left him behind, he was six years old. Only six. With Ma far away. And then there was his marriage, which Baba arranged in a tearing hurry. After Didi and me, Mejo was Baba's third match-making victim. Baba never seemed to learn.

Here's what happened. My aunt's husband had found this girl, but she was way over the hill. He knew her family, and was eager to push the match through for Mejo. So he got Baba good and drunk the day he was to go see her. That's how they extracted Baba's word. Now, Mejo wouldn't have known about this. But on the day Baba went for the final-word ceremony, he invited my husband to go along. Baba had realised by then that he'd been tricked into agreeing, but as before, he was doggedly bound by his word. He took my husband along, thinking that since he's brainless, he won't notice that the girl is no fresh jasmine. My husband may be dim, but he's not blind. He saw what there was to see. After they got back to the village, Mejo cornered him. He knew that the others may finesse the truth, but my husband simply couldn't. When Mejo grilled him, he spilled the beans: 'Ffff, I wasn't too fond of the girl. Her face is weird. She's probably older than you. And dark on top of that. I don't know what Baba was thinking.' Mejo, of course, was livid.

See, there was a bit of a back story. Mejo was friends with a woman in the village who was married and a mother of three. They were probably more than friends. Baba was naturally worried. That was part of his hurry. And Mejo had come around to moving on from this relationship. But strapped to an old maid? He never forgave Baba.

Baba knew that Mejo had found out and was fearful that he might try to escape. On the wedding day, the groom's party started out towards the bride's house with my Kaka in charge as the lead groomsman. Baba pulled Kaka aside and said, 'Stay with Mejo. Don't let him out of sight. And remember, the Dhola crossing is not safe, there are often bandits lurking there. There are all these women decked in jewellery. Be careful.' On this side of the Dhola crossing, Mejo told Kaka that he needed to go poo. Maybe it was not a ruse. He knew he was trapped, maybe his tummy did in fact rumble. But Kaka had Baba's brief, he was sure that Mejo was going to go behind the bushes and then make a run for it. He very sweetly stalled Mejo: 'Hold it in for just a little bit, babu? See, we're close to the Dhola crossing. This is a really risky spot. And we have all these women in the party. We don't have that much farther to go. And there are loos where we're going, you'll see.' Mejo couldn't get away.

The wedding happened. I was there, I could see how furious Mejo was. I could also see that the bride looked leathery, like a mango once ripe but now dry.

I tried to pacify Mejo: 'Look, much of this was written on your forehead. Besides, she's not so bad. You two will be like same-age friends. And as for her looks, if you had to work the field in the sun like village folks, you would look far worse. Since we live in the city, we've gotten used to lacy looks.'

Mejo briefly perked up, 'Really Mej-di, you think it'll work out?'

I said, 'Absolutely.'

Baba had expected Mejo to settle down in the house he had built in the village. He arranged Mejo's wedding a few years after his return. I'm sure he was thinking, 'At least one son will stay with me.' And Mejo might have been fine with that. He was a village man. The rest of us were raised in the city. But Baba's disastrous match-making soured Mejo and scuttled this plan.

After his marriage, Mejo had initially kept his wife at arm's length. He eventually came around to accepting her and built a family. But in doing so, he became increasingly venomous towards us. Mostly towards Baba, but also Ma and the siblings. He is bitter to this day, nearly twenty years after Baba's passing. Just the other day, he called Choto to threaten him. 'Just like I took Haldar'—lately he makes it sound like he killed Baba, although he never calls him Baba—'just like I took Haldar, I'll take you too. You won't get away.' Empty threats, of course. He's delusional.

But there's something I have to confess. See, Mejo's wife was from a village well-known for black magic. For the first few months of his marriage, Mejo was still going with that other woman and completely ignoring his wife. One day, I went to her and said, 'There are so many different spells that folks in your village must know about. Can't you find something that'll peel Mejo away from her and towards you?' I never found out what she did, if anything. But within a month, Mejo had broken up with the other woman. Around the same time, his bitterness towards our family began to bloom. Was there a connection? Did this eventually lead him to attack Baba? I'll never know.

# 14

# Shelf Life

'Thakuma is dying,' Buttermilk said absently one morning. Karno's mother was finally taking her leave at nearly a hundred. She had outlived both Karno and Bashona. Now refusing food, she lay shrivelled in her cot, shooing away gathering family: 'Don't crowd me, my parents are here.'

'You know, Thakuma birthed all my three children,' Buttermilk reminisced. She wove in how Bashona's grandmother had similarly birthed her, as her mother-in-law did her daughters' children—nearly fifty years apart. 'They take a slip of green bamboo, slice off slivers and smear them with a liquid. It's a tea made of some roots and leaves. All midwives have it. Those slivers are really sharp, no less than knives, maybe more. I know they cut with steel in the hospitals now. But you know, bamboo, it has no disease.' She recalled her first birth: 'Thakuma cut the cord with the bamboo sliver and handed me my baby. But I gave her money first. Ma had taught me. You put money on the midwife's palm before taking the baby. That's the rule.'

'We don't burn our dead like most Hindus,' said Buttermilk, back from Thakuma's funeral. 'We bury them. It's a family promise to Panchu Thakur.' Panchu Thakur—the saviour of children—belongs in the pantheon of folk gods of the Sunderbans, where a rich vein of animist and nature worship runs apace with more mainstream religious practices. 'But this is only on Baba's side,' she said, to clarify the spottiness of the burial practice. 'Ma's family burns their dead. But a woman once married belongs in her husband's family. So we buried Ma, naturally.'

'Where do you bury?'

'Oh, on the banks of our Ganga.'

'But your village doesn't have a river,' I reminded her.

'Tsk,' she clucked at my pickiness. 'It's a lake. But huge. Say, you walked along your lane, turned on the main road, went all the way to Golpark, and came back around. That much.' A couple of acres. A large water body touched by the eternal, hence Ganga. 'On one bank is the crematorium, where open pyres are lit. On the other bank is the burial ground.'

'How big is this burial ground?'

'About the size of this lot on which your house stands.' That would be 4,000 square feet, which sounded shockingly small.

'How can such a tiny ground serve an entire village?'

'Fff, one village?' she scoffed. 'More like forty or fifty villages. People come from far, far away.'

'So they are all on top of each other?' I was struck, finally dislodged from my fixed notion of a graveyard, with its inefficient land use.

'Of course they are,' she said, as if restating the obvious. 'When burying Baba, we came upon seven skulls! Those teeth and eye sockets …' she trailed off, unsettled by the memory.

The diggers open up a hole wide enough for the body and about three feet deep. Fresh burials are easy to spot and avoided. I wondered about coffins. 'We don't use boxes,' Buttermilk put that to rest. 'Even the Muslims don't put the box in, they reuse it. Much like our cots. Do the Hindus burn funerary cots? No, right? I've seen Christian burials, even they won't put in the box. On the fresh mound, where we leave a terracotta urn, they'll stick an arrow.' She made a cross with her fingers. 'But you know what the real difference is? The Muslims have a festival for visiting their dead. They go to the burial ground, place flowers, remember their ancestors, leave offerings in their name. So do the Christians. Us Hindus, we'll stick them in the ground and never return. For us, the person is not in that spot.' This did sound very Hindu: instead of ashes in a cremation, the body becomes earth in a burial; the site attracts no memorial attachment.

But few truths in India are absolute. 'Some people leave instructions about home burial,' Buttermilk continued. 'In these cases, a dais is built on the grave, sometimes even a small structure. There, every day at dusk, you light an oil lamp and incense, place flowers, sugar offerings and water. Not doing this can bring the family misfortune.' This brought her back to Thakuma's burial. 'My Thakurda wanted Thakuma to be buried at home, right next to him. So that's what we did. We dug a hole and laid it with brick and mortar. We even made a little cement pillow for her. They lay her down, covered her with earth, then sealed it with cement. There'll be a small temple on it later. Thakurda has one. The two will be side by side. In their own yard.'

'If anyone asks us, we say we are ghoti Koiborto.' Describing Thakuma's funeral had led Buttermilk to talk about her caste. The prefix 'ghoti' says that her ancestors have always lived in West Bengal. They did not ride in, like my family did in 1948, on one of the many waves of dispossessed humanity from the east. These migrations, like a subcontinental tic, followed every spasm of sectarian violence starting in 1947, past 1971, and into the '90s. Koiborto—the farmer caste—is the single largest in West Bengal today, covering an estimated third of the state's population. This caste is not high in the hierarchy, neither is it low. It is an Other Backward Caste (OBC)—that sibilant me-too category in India's affirmative action rigmarole. But Buttermilk's family lives outside the ambit of OBC reservations and its primarily urban benefits. 'We've always been farmers,' she said. 'I've never heard anyone get into any sort of trade or business. We work the land. At most open a rice vend, like Baba tried to do. But he didn't really succeed. The only exception is my brother Choto. He's done well as a textile trader. But he didn't get that from the family. He struck out alone.'

India's caste hierarchy is like the operating system that undergirds a computer. Crucial but largely dormant, it lurks for the right signals to get fired up. The funeral is one such scenario, when caste practices come to the fore. But the most prominent, undoubtedly, is marriage; no shelf in the caste hierarchy, high or low, is immune to its demands. Marriages, especially in rural India, are still largely arranged by parents. Buttermilk has had to navigate these caste waters in marrying all three of her children.

There are rules of thumb in a marriage liaison. A woman, once married, acquires her husband's caste. Since elevation of caste is always desirable, you look to marry your daughter at or above your caste, unless there's a damaging attribute that needs to be offset. Things didn't quite work out this way for Buttermilk's eldest, Rikta.

'My son-in-law's surname is Noshkor,' said Buttermilk, as if sharing a chronic illness. The last name usually bears the caste stamp, but I couldn't read this one, likely due to my own high-caste vantage. 'They are Pod, a really low caste,' she explained, 'These folks sell fruits and veggies. Remember Prodeep, the guy you buy your veggies from? He's a Noshkor. And Batulda, the green coconut vendor who sings? Him too.'

But this match was complicated. Rikta's husband, Sumit Noshkor, was an educated man with a white-collar job, lower in caste but much higher in class than Buttermilk. His family had been dead against this match. Not because of Rikta, who was then an attractive twenty-year-old with a high-school degree. But because of Buttermilk's maid work. 'You know who came to see Rikta for the match? Sumit! He came alone.' In an arranged match, it is highly unusual to solicit oneself, unaccompanied by family elders. 'He also went to my village and met the family. Everybody loved him. He's tall and esmaat.' Smart. 'Then we went to see his family: me, my sister-in-law and her husband. I didn't say yes. As we were leaving, Sumit grabbed my sister-in-law's hands and broke down in tears: Aunty, please convince Ma, this is the one I want to marry! So, they worked on me on the auto ride home: the boy is a diamond chip, why are you being so stubborn? I said: these people are low caste, I'll say yes, and then later won't everyone blame me? They countered, saying there are Noshkors even in our caste.'

Buttermilk eventually relented and her fears came to pass. 'As the wedding proceeded my in-laws' family saw the rituals. And they knew.' The caste practices had surged into light. 'After the wedding they tore the roof off heaping blame on me. But Rikta let them have it: "My father is broken, my mother has raised us alone spitting blood, did you ever stand by her? Whoever she's chosen for me is the best." And to me she said: "Whose happiness make you happy? The family's or mine? If it's the latter, then let me tell you that I'm very happy." And you know, they really are perfect together. They had a daughter, Moumita, within the first year. Sumit is more than my own son now. I can put my weight on him. The crack with my extended family over this never healed. But Rikta's success makes it all worthwhile.'

Bonomali was a bigger challenge. 'The first time I married him off he was only seventeen and the bride was fourteen,' Buttermilk sighed. Those ages are quite a bit below what is legally sanctioned. 'It's a long story, maybe I'll tell you another time. I was under a lot of pressure. Bonomali had become a wasted druggie, out of control.' It was naturally hard to find a match for such a groom. But any damage can be offset by sliding down the caste ladder. Buttermilk had to reach deep. 'Her name was Bhokti. Beautiful she was. Fair, with big black eyes. Like an angel.' Buttermilk became misty-eyed. 'She was from the Kaora caste, as low as can be. They work with fish and meat. Even pork. We don't pay heed to this anymore, but they are what used to be called untouchables.'

I had never cracked the *Manu Samhita* before—that text, a couple thousand years old, which codifies India's caste hierarchy in lurid detail. Much of the text hovers on the top rung: the Brahmins, custodians of the hierarchy. But there it was, chapter 10 verse 36: 'Karavar (or Kaora) are butchers and leatherworkers, they will live outside the village.' Buttermilk hadn't read these words. Neither have many literate Indians. But everybody knows them, up and down the caste ladder.

'When Bhokti walked out with their baby, Bonomali was

destroyed,' Buttermilk continued, 'but I waited a few years before marrying him again. I tried to fix him first.' She sent him to rehab, taking on extra shifts to pay for it. 'Then I brought in Rupa, you've seen her. She is a Pramanik, from the barber caste. Much lower than us, although not as low as the Kaora. But then she was a divorcee.' Bonomali, between his drug problem and a failed marriage, was by now a seriously compromised candidate. But a divorced woman's marriage prospects are worse. In Rupa, Buttermilk had pulled off a rather fine-tuned match.

'My younger daughter, Mamata, was a different story.' Mamata's husband, Sukhendu Hajra, is an overseer at a factory, with land in his village. 'He is a Gop. This is the milkman caste. The same level as us. And he's a lovely boy, just like Sumit. Everyone says my sons-in-law are gems! Mamata's is the best match of the four I've made for my three children.' But it came after considerable grief and delay. 'I started looking when Mamata was twenty-one. You know how old she was when I finally married her? Twenty-six!' Practically an old maid in Buttermilk's books.

Mamata had a high school degree, like Rikta, and was a trained seamstress. It was her skin colour that got in the way. 'She has her father's colour, not mine,' explained Buttermilk, who is caramel to Jhoro's dark chocolate. In a country with every skin tone from alabaster to coal, the shade card is a crucial factor in the marriage market. Fair skin can offset handicaps in caste or class. 'They would come to see her—god knows how many parties over those five years—and leave saying the same thing: too dark.' As news of this unfolding failure spread, her Subhashgram neighbours circled, like so many sharks in freshly bloodied waters. Buttermilk would leave for work. But Mamata was home alone all day, riddled with repeated rejections, her anxieties exposed like open veins.

'If something happens in a flat like yours, the word stays in, unless you let it out,' Buttermilk pointed out. 'But the way we live, news has its own life. It travels fast and bloats up along the way. Like a corpse.' Buttermilk wishes for privacy in her life; she would like to be able to exercise her right to be left alone. None of the Indian languages have a word for privacy, secrecy is the closest one can get. This fact has often been used against privacy advocates in India, which has no privacy laws. The argument being: since the languages don't support it, privacy must be an elite import. Buttermilk has had no import opportunities.

The prying neighbours, always women, would typically target Mamata's advancing age. For example: 'Eh Ma, you're turning into a basket of loofahs! Who'll take you?' Buttermilk decoded this for me: 'You know how old women's breasts hang, like dried ridge-gourds on the vine.' Or, 'Hay hay, this girl's all bagasse now!' Buttermilk explained: 'Old flesh is a fibrous chew; young flesh melts in the mouth.' These vicious taunts cut Mamata to shreds. But she kept it from Buttermilk, leaning instead on her sister. 'She would call Rikta and cry: "Didi, they say these horrible things! If Ma would find me even a rickshawallah, I would go. I can't bear it anymore!" Rikta only shared this with me after Mamata's marriage. They knew I was doing my best and didn't want me to worry. Imagine, such gems I have for daughters!'

It wasn't only the prospective grooms who rejected Mamata; Buttermilk rejected a few prospectives herself. 'This was towards the end, when we were all getting desperate. Sumit brought news of a match. A huge three-storey house, a coal vend, a cattle-feed vend. And a lot of land besides. So we went. The house was fine, if a little unfinished. The boy was working in the field. When he came

in, I was stunned. I pulled Sumit aside and said: "This is a disaster!"
The boy was not a boy at all, but a wiry old man! His front teeth
were all missing. When he spoke, his tongue wanted to escape,
like a bird! Phurut, phurut!' Buttermilk giggled at the memory and
then turned stony: 'My Baba married me off looking at the land
and not the boy. I wasn't about to make the same mistake.' There
were others. 'One boy was young, but dark as sin. And four times
the addict my Bonomali is. His eyes were like hot coals! Babbah re,
the tunnel was long and harsh. But it led to Sukhendu.'

Mamata, now happily married, was desperate for a child. It had
been four years. 'Every month, the day she starts her periods, she'll
call me and cry,' said Buttermilk. Tests had traced the problem to
Mamata. She'd been on medication but that hadn't helped. 'Now
the doctor is asking for another raft of tests: lots of blood work,
ultrasound, and who knows what else. Tell me, won't this cost a
fortune? My poor Sukhendu makes 8,000 rupees a month.' I was
worried that Mamata's reproductive melancholia could irreparably
damage their finances. Had they considered adoption? 'Absolutely
not,' Buttermilk batted the idea away. 'Is your own blood the same
as another's? It never works.' She had a different solution. 'I want to
take her to Bojurki Baba's thaan.' A Shiva temple in the Sunderbans.
'Childless women go there in droves. Most have had their laps filled.
But Mamata won't go. She's been to school, you see, she believes in
the doctor. All this is village mumbo-jumbo, she thinks.' Buttermilk
looked crestfallen. 'What can I do? I'll go on her behalf, for my
own peace.'

Another menstrual cycle later, however, Mamata's rationalist
resolve had given way. She and Rupa—both in the throes of

motherhood fever—accompanied Buttermilk to Bojurki. This fertility temple is deep in the delta, where the land dissolves into a water filigree. Small and worn, its ancient walls bear remnants of ornamental plasterwork. Next to the Shiva temple is one to his consort Kali, she of the lolling tongue. The two stand in a shady compound on the banks of a lake, its waters still and dark. It is here that the science-minded Mamata submitted to the spirit world.

Buttermilk came back from the temple jubilant. She had seen all the signs. 'We went on a full moon Monday, ideal for Shiva,' she explained. 'So there was a terribly long line of women.' When your turn comes, you sit in front of the lingam, the priest places a flower on it and extends his caste thread in a loop. Ideally, the flower drops from the tip of the phallus onto the waiting caste thread below. The scene had left Buttermilk rapt. 'I wouldn't have believed it if I hadn't seen it myself! Look, I'm getting goosebumps now. Mamata didn't see a thing. Her head was bowed and she was sobbing anyway. But I looked. There was the flower, trembling like something alive. And then it fell, toop! Straight onto the loop!' There was more. 'You need to bathe in the lake before the ritual. Mamata and Rupa had just bathed, and the three of us had gathered under a bael tree in the yard.' Bael, or wood apple, is believed to be Shiva's favourite fruit. 'Right then, a ripe bael fell on Mamata's back and rolled away behind her, into the waiting hands of an old beggar! Seeing this, the whole crowd erupted! "Nothing can stop you now," they all said. "Baba has himself planted a bael within you!"' Rupa's case was less clear. 'The crowd was pushing and shoving,' Buttermilk said, 'I think the flower dropped for Rupa too, but I couldn't see it. Somebody got in the way just then. I did see that the flower didn't tremble for her.'

I tried telling Buttermilk that flowers dripping from a stone phallus, however graphic, couldn't possibly have anything to do with pregnancy. Her worldview was more inclusive. 'The doctors got several years,' she said with a centred smile, 'now the gods should get a chance.'

Just shy of nine months from this temple visit, Mamata gave birth to a bonny daughter. Rupa, on the other hand, continued to bear her childlessness and sank into a deeper funk.

'We're going back to Bojurki,' declared Buttermilk, 'want to come?' Mamata's daughter, Shruti, was now at six months. It was time to pay the gods back for this much-yearned child.

On her last visit, Mamata had made a promise to the Kali at Bojurki: fill my lap and I'll bleed my heart for you. In practice, this is less dramatic. 'We'll make a small nick on her left chest with a razor blade,' Buttermilk explained, 'then wipe the place with a bael leaf to catch a drop of blood or two.' That leaf is then ceremonially offered to the goddess. Shiva, on the other hand, was owed the child's birth hair and first nail clippings. The gods would receive their payment in blood and hair and nail to a deafening crescendo of drums and gongs. Buttermilk had invited over thirty family members to witness this. There would be a feast afterwards. Jhoro was bringing their own Morichshali puffed rice from the village, Rikta was bringing onion fritters, and Buttermilk was going to cook an enormous vat of ghoogni, a rich stew of yellow peas and potatoes. This was a major celebration, weeks in the planning. The only off note was Rupa. 'She can't stop crying,' Buttermilk looked wrenched. 'Tell me, is this in my hands? I told her: "See, this child is in my daughter's family, she doesn't belong to me. My son's child

is mine. And that party I'll throw with twice as much dhoom-
dhaam! I promise." What else can I say?'

The date for the event was a careful choice. 'Shiva wants the
hair and nail before the baby's first-rice ceremony, which is in ten
days,' she explained. 'And it must be given on a Monday, because
Shiva. Want to come?' she repeated.

I really wanted to but was occupied on that date. As consolation
I used Buttermilk's directions and Google's satellite view to
zoom in on the temple compound. Buttermilk, peering over my
shoulders, was thrilled that this was possible: 'There, that's the lake
and those are the temples!' A pause. 'Wait, the Shiva temple looks
right, but it doesn't have a grille around it like this one.' I suggested
it had probably appeared in the fifteen months since her last visit.

She took the Monday off and came to work on Tuesday,
exhausted but awash in a post-project glow. 'It all went as
planned,' she said with a happy sigh, 'except five people didn't
show. But if they had, I would've been in trouble. I nearly ran
out of ghoogni. Village folks can sure scarf down a lot. But then
moori-ghoogni is all I was feeding them.' Her chatter stopped,
she remembered something: 'You know what? There really is a
grille now. You were right.'

Buttermilk had singlehandedly managed this event, from
funds to invitations. In addition, she had kept her own promise
to the gods for this child: circumambulate the Shiva temple in an
inchworm body crawl. Sprawl on the ground, face down, arms
outstretched. Draw yourself up and stand where your fingertips
were. Repeat. She needed about seventy body-lengths to cover the
circumference. With her guests watching. 'I went around once,
and thought: let me keep going. So I went around once more,'
she said. 'Now my thighs feel like lead. I'm going to have to skip

laundry today.' She continued: 'Seeing me, Mamata went around once. Then Bonomali went three times. He kept praying: turn two into four.' Bonomali was asking god to give him and Rupa two children. His crawl was not a debt payment, but a promissory note. He inchwormed along in the midday heat, watched by his emotionally wrecked wife.

'If I'd known beforehand what time I'd be crawling, I'd have told you,' Buttermilk said, her face tinged with regret. 'And you could've watched me do it.'

'But how?' I was befuddled.

'Why, the same way you showed me the temple and the grille!'

It took me a moment to figure this out: she thought what I had shown her on Google was some sort of CCTV feed from the temple. If you can see the temple from your desk, you must be seeing it live. A very good theory. More striking was her regret at my failure to witness her body crawl.

Buttermilk had become accustomed to her life's grains being gathered. She didn't want them to go unattended anymore.

# 15

# Monsoon Crop '15

'We got flooded to death this boro harvest,' Buttermilk had said, 'Maybe we'll be dried to death during the next amon planting.' Her words from mid-May turned out to be prescient. June brought a historic heatwave, killing over 2,000 people nationwide in the first week. The monsoon had been delayed. The earth was packed hard. Pre-monsoon showers, essential to unleashing the grass that nourishes the soil, were nowhere in sight. But the planting couldn't wait; the seeds had to go in. Farmers had to take on the extra burden of irrigating and fertilising their amon seedbeds. This came on the back of a damaged boro harvest, so wet that the grain had partially germinated, making it unfit for market.

'We're eating our boro rice this year,' sighed Buttermilk, 'and therefore husking all of it.' The grain is ordinarily sold as paddy. She was just back from a husking trip to the village. 'A ton of work! Ouf!' The paddy is first soaked for a couple of days, then placed in large vats and partially steamed. 'Not a lot of water and not a full boil, mind you. This is halfway.' The grain is then spread out in the sun to dry. 'This is the trickiest bit. You can't use the harsh midday sun. Say you spread it out in the morning, when the light is soft. You then need to flip it every fifteen minutes or so. Scrape the grains up and spread them out again. It's a pain.' The paddy is then picked up and soaked again and placed into vats, this time piled high. 'In this second round, you cook it on high heat until the husks begin to smoke. Then you dry the grain again, to a crisp this time, in the hottest sun. Only now are the husks ready to come off. Back in the day, everybody had husking rams at home. Now it's all machines. But even that's not the end of the story.' The husked rice is full of chaff and needs to be winnowed. 'You scoop up the rice on bamboo trays and fling it in the air until the chaff blows off. Batch after batch. Until your arms grow heavy. That's what it takes to turn paddy into rice. Bujhecho?'

Buttermilk had been tutoring me on rice for some time. But on this occasion, she pivoted away from production into territory we had not touched before. 'Husking with the ram used to be backbreaking work,' she said. 'But compare that rice with the machine-husked stuff? The sky and the netherworld! You would inhale a whole plateful simply with salt and green chillies. Such depth!' She spoke of taste, holding forth like a fussy foodie: rice, when done right, stood on its own; it wasn't just a bed for curries to pose on. She recited names of local strains, now lost: 'Talmugur, Ponkai, Lokkhideeghol, Rawtnomukhi …' These were common even a couple decades ago, before large agro businesses captured the rural seed markets. 'There was this one called Kalomuthi.' She was in the throes of nostalgia. 'Sweet as can be, and so fragrant! You would sniff your hand for hours afterwards. And striking to look at too! Black husk, red rice.' Evidently high in nutrients. 'I would love to do a Kalomuthi planting again if I could get my hands on some seeds. I was telling my husband just the other day.'

Bengal once had over 5,000 native strains of rice. About 1,000 remain in seed banks, a majority no longer active cultivars. Buttermilk's yearning for another Kalomuthi crop was propelled by taste memory. Untrammelled by all that life had thrown at her, it was a foodie's quest to eat well. Rice producers are naturally its most discerning consumers. If debt and hunger don't get in the way.

Buttermilk continued on the issue of milled rice: 'The thing is, everyone now wants everything pheresh.' Fresh. 'The body, the face—don't they make the skin pheresh by rubbing creams?' There is indeed an epidemic of fairness creams in India. 'The same with rice. So, you're running a husking machine, fine. But you won't run it once, will you? Getting the husk off is not enough. You'll run it until the skin on the grain is entirely peeled.' This takes the rice bran with it, which is not lost in manual husking. Buttermilk doesn't know about the bran and its nutritional value, but the taste differential is bright on her tongue. 'And even that is not enough. You're going to apply powder to make the grain look even whiter! Say a wholesale rice buyer arrives at the grain market. He'll pick a handful of rice from a random sack'—she made a scoop with her hand, rooting air—'not from the top, but from deep within. He then splays it out on the floor. Now he inspects the grains. Broken, black, splotched, veined. These are all imperfections. The grain vendor fights them with powder. Just like the father of a dark girl would for prospective in-laws!' Buttermilk clapped her hands and cracked up at her own joke.

This dolled-up version is what I usually buy at the store: milled and bleached rice, sealed in a bag.

We had entered the third week of June. No rain. Brain-curdling heat.

'I see sheets in the laundry basket,' Buttermilk said, 'but I won't do them today.'

'Why not?' It had been a week since her husking trip. Were her arms still sore?

'My arms are fine.' She giggled at my ignorance. 'It's Ombubachi! Can't hit the earth for three days.'

Ombubachi—derived from the Sanskrit Ambuvaci, literally, the start of the waters—is an annual ritual observed widely in Bengal and Assam at the opening of the monsoons. It begins on the seventh day of the Bengali month of Ashadh, 22 June, by when the rains have arrived in earnest. The faithful believe that the earth renews itself at this time by menstruating for three days, and therefore needs privacy and rest. Deities are screened off in their shrines. Digging or pounding the earth are taboo.

My flat is up on the third floor, technically not within the Ombubachi purview. By refusing to pound laundry, Buttermilk had brought me down to earth, within the ambit of her antenna permanently tuned to the land and its seasons.

'This time of year, you send gifts of mango and jackfruit to the homes of married daughters,' she shared. The prolonged heat had flooded the markets with fruit, lowering prices. 'At least one good came of it! My husband has already delivered the gift hampers to Mamata and Rikta. Rupa's parents have sent one to me. I can't just accept that empty-handed, of course. I have to send them something in return.' Such gifts exchanges go on year-round. 'In the winter, you send nolen gur at Mawkor Shonkranti. That's mid-January.' Buttermilk counted them on her fingers. 'For Choitro Shonkranti, you send crushed moori, gram flour and hunks of sugar-palm sap dried into bars. That's mid-April. It's mango-jackfruit for the Ashadh new moon, towards the end of June. For Durga Pujo, you have to send clothes by early October.' These were the major giving occasions. There were many others. 'For example, in early July, for Rawth, you send chinir mawth.' Mini sculptures of solid sugar, typically of spired temples. 'At Jonmashtomi, usually the end of August, you send taaler bawra.' Fritters made from the glutinous orange flesh of the sugar-palm fruit. 'The list goes on. Plus, you always send fruits, whatever's seasonal. What else are in-laws for?'

For her monsoon planting the previous year, Buttermilk had contended with armed thugs on her land. That threat had since subsided, owing to the meeting hosted by the village elder. This year's troubles were brewing not on land but in the skies. After a bone-dry June, it was as if July had thrown a switch. Sheets of rain lashed the land. This was welcome news for now. It was time to break the seedbeds and replant the saplings in prepared paddies. Standing water is what the farmer wanted. Up to a point.

'This rain is for goch-punno, which is tomorrow. It's all set up, you see.' Buttermilk was confident about nature's clock. Goch-punno is the ceremonial planting of the first bundle of saplings. The saplings had been transported from the seedbed to the paddies in bundles of fifty, dangling from bamboo yokes.

Before the workers got started, Jhoro, as the owner, would wade in, cup up some water and sprinkle it in all four directions while saying a prayer, then plant a bundle of saplings himself. 'This has to be on a Monday, because Shiva. If he's not happy he can flood all the three realms.' Buttermilk had hired twenty men to work her ditch. 'Like I said, it's all set up. Today, Sunday, the new moon leaves. Tomorrow is goch-punno, followed by two days of intense planting. Wednesday is Rawth for us and Eid for the Muslims. You'll see, that's when the skies will really open up. And won't stop until Ultorawth, a week later. That's what makes for happy paddy.' Reciting this clockwork schedule, she knew, was really a prayer. 'If god wants to keep us, this is what he'll do. And if he wants to kill us, he'll hold the water now and release it all later. That's all there is to it.'

Since the crop relies entirely on the rains, monsoon planting is a highly optimised business. 'It is best to get the planting done by early July, because the days are still long.' The summer solstice had passed two weeks before. 'And the heaviest rains are ahead. The saplings need to steady up in order to use the real downpour.' The farmer is tuned to expect not just the volume of water, but a particular distribution. Buttermilk provided a succinct list of ways in which the skies could make short work of her amon rice. 'If the rains are heavy with no dry stretches, the ears of rice get buggy and drop off. If a storm blows in, it can snap the rice stems and finish things off. And a flood, of course, takes it all away. The sky has a whole arsenal. The game has just begun. Let's see what happens.'

It was early July, the thick of Ashadh. Rural Bengal was in the throes of the biggest rice planting of the year. Tens of millions of farmers had their eyes trained on the sky. Not that this was news.

The papers were abuzz with a deadly ISIS attack at an upscale restaurant in Dhaka.

The raised aisle snaked through acres of paddies pocked with rain. Up close it had a generous icing of mud, on which Buttermilk plodded carefully. Her slippers had each become a tricky skate. The world around was grey: a flabby sky fused with its reflection below, the horizon blotted by rain. Wind-whipped, her broken umbrella looked like a damaged bird. The rain fell with a steady hiss, thankfully not a torrent. She was en route to supervising planting work on her land. Jhoro had taken ill.

Buttermilk's fears turned out to be well-founded. Only six of the twenty appointed workers had shown up. Her presence caused a flurry, and within half an hour a few more hands had gathered. But she was pleased with the progress so far. Her planting was ahead of most because she had been able to break her seedbeds early. There were issues, however. The standing water in her ditch teemed with what looked like gobs of phlegm. These were nasty bugs, common this time of year. They close in on the saplings strangling them and severely hurt the yield—a single plant per sapling where there might be a clump of eight or ten. She had her workers fish the bugs out with nets, but some inevitably clung on. She would need to spring for pesticides and hire a sprayer to properly take care of this. Standing on the muddy aisle, soaked to the bone, the thought exhausted Buttermilk. She decided not to bother. All of this was just to hold on to her land. Had she been a full-time farmer, she would've fought for a better crop.

It rained incessantly. July ended with nearly twice the normal volume of rain, the wettest in a decade. City life was thrown out of gear. My freshly painted walls developed depressing damp spots. In Buttermilk's Subhashgram home, the porch took on water for the first time. They had to move the stove and cooking gear off the ground and onto a cot, which became the makeshift kitchen. No one in her home was getting much sleep. Her commute to work had turned horrific. The path to Subhashgram station was a sea of mud. And in the village, the standing water in the paddies crept up all month long, turning from friend to foe in a slow betrayal. On the heels of the disastrous boro harvest, this year's amon planting was ravaged by floods.

'There's nearly three feet of standing water on my ditch,' Buttermilk said, looking like she had taken one on the chin. Ever the optimist, she had found a redeeming feature: 'The phlegm bugs were all washed away, though. And the water is really clear. You can see the saplings, they're this high,' she extended her right palm and touched below the wrist with her left hand. About eight inches. A tragic underwater tableau.

The rains continued. The skies had delivered the annual monsoon quota by the end of August, in two months instead of the usual four. Nearly all of rural Bengal was reeling. September was abnormally rainless. As the land dried, the state doled out flood relief: seeds for a fresh planting and 3,000 rupees per farmer. Buttermilk did not qualify for this, because she could not prove that her land was hers. Instead, she improvised.

'Remember the paddies had clear floodwater,' she said, with the glint of one who'd found a chink in the armour. 'That's something Baba had taught me.' If the floodwater is murky, it has brought in mud that settles on the submerged saplings over time. They eventually keel over under the weight and cannot be revived. Buttermilk's saplings stayed up because of clear rainwater. 'Everyone said, throw them out and start over. But I thought: come what may, I can't take on more losses. God's whip stings harder than man's. I left the planting alone. When the water went down, I just sprinkled the mud with dried dung to boost the soil. By the time the earth dried to a crust, the saplings had grown out four or five knuckles.' Rice, like bamboo, belongs to the grass family. Left alone, it gains height punctuated by knuckles that give off roots. 'If you snap off the top knuckle and replant that, it multiplies into a thick clump. That's what everyone advised me to do. But I didn't want the additional labour cost.' She simply replanted the overgrown and knuckled saplings in mid-September.

Two months went by. On a cool November morning, Buttermilk came to work with news.

'The grains have filled with milk!' she burst out, her thrill barely contained.

'What milk?'

'Oh, you don't know about this.' She slowed down: 'We've just finished Kartik and entered Awghran'—Awghran is the Bengali month from mid-November to mid-December—'which is when the rice grains get filled. If you press one, milk squirts out.'

'So it hardens later?' I had no idea.

'Yes, yes,' she said impatiently, 'but there's more. You know how I plant fat grain in my ditch and skinny grain in the others?' I did remember: the fat grain was Morichshali, for puffed rice, and the skinny was Dudhershawr. 'Usually, the fat grain gets milky by the middle of Kartik and the skinny by the start of Awghran.'

There was that clockwork schedule again, tattooed on her farmer psyche. 'This year's planting was so messy that I had no idea what to expect. I had my husband check the fat grain at the end of October. Nothing. I was worried sick. Then I just heard yesterday that the fat grains have filled up! Two weeks late, but wasn't the planting horribly delayed?' She was radiant with relief. 'I'll have an amon harvest yet!'

Her flooded and knuckled saplings had not let her down.

Buttermilk's euphoria at her grain's survival was short-lived. It was like a tic that the land in her blood had wired her for. By mid-December, with the grain ripe in the field, the cold reality of yet another hobbled harvest had set in.

'The cutting begins tomorrow, I've hired all these hands,' she looked harried. 'This is just the start. I'm going to be bleeding money for the next two weeks.' Meanwhile, she had heard that grain prices had fallen. 'I lost all that money in the boro harvest. And now for the amon I won't even make half my money back. It's the same every time. How long can I can keep doing this?' Something in her had shifted, her pathological optimism breached. 'I carry this around like a stone, you know, right here,' she pressed the middle of her chest. 'It's a dull ache. Never goes away. I try and forget it. Like I'm talking with you now, feeling lighter. I'm telling others too. As I talk, the ache waits, crouched like a black bird. Not too far from me. As soon as I'm alone, it pounces back to feed on my heart.'

What was this thing that she carried around? Perhaps it was the fault line between her farmer genes and her circumstances. By the end of the amon harvest, her mounting losses had finally beaten

Buttermilk. She would have to sit out the following boro crop. 'I don't fight humans,' she laughed, lighter after the wrenching decision. 'My fights are all with god. But I haven't seen him. If I did, I would wring his little neck. Neither have I seen the shorkaar. I would tear its hair off for never taking my side.'

But this was all in jest, a camouflaged assertion that she lived her trapeze act alone, with no safety net from god or country.

16

# Guilt

Back-to-back crop failures had left Buttermilk flaccid, like a rubber band stretched one too many times. As I began to worry that she may not bounce back, she revealed an unexpected tack in coping with her troubles: 'Do you know why my life is cursed this way? Why my crops fail, my son goes to waste, my husband keeps falling ill? It's punishment for something I did.'

It is July 2005. Bonomali is sixteen. He and his pals hang out on a cracked culvert in Subhashgram. They're smoking pot. None of them go to school. They work labouring jobs when they can get them. The day is overcast, a break between drizzles. A girl walks by. The boys know her, she's from the neighbourhood. Always easy on the eye, she looks extra pretty today. What's the occasion? 'Ei Puchu, take us with you!' they let out a collective catcall. 'She's walking to her wedding,' one boy offers. This makes the group dissolve into raucous cackles. Puchu, in the long tradition of subcontinental women, ignores them. As the giggles subside and the emptiness creeps back, one boy airs an idea: 'I bet none of you could run up and touch Puchu.' This energises the group and quickly escalates into a bone-headed wager. 'I'll pay fifty rupees,' one says, the price of several hits. None of them are up to the challenge, so they gang up on the weakling. Bonomali, his usual dimness furthered by dope, gets roped in.

The skies open up the next day, the monsoons are in full flow. Buttermilk's Subhashgram courtyard has a foot of standing water. From the low-lying plot next door, a stream of red crabs skitter into her property seeking higher ground. Telo kankra, they're called, palm crabs. Unlike the large ocean crab Buttermilk had caught as a child, these are palm-sized. As they sidle by, Bonomali plucks them with little whoops of delight. He loves eating crabs, just like his mother. He has no recollection of what he's done the day before. When the drizzle lets up and a crowd shows up at the gate asking for him, he walks up willingly. Even seeing Puchu in the group doesn't ring a bell.

Buttermilk was just back from work. Mamata, who still lived at home, alerted her to a commotion outside. She emerged to a chilling scene: Puchu had grabbed Bonomali by the hair, pulling his head down, while her mother, sister and other relatives rained blows on him. Buttermilk had no idea what her son had done, and worse, neither did he. Puchu's family alleged sexual assault. Buttermilk pressed Bonomali hoping for some traction: did he really do what he was being accused of, or was Puchu cooking it up? Bonomali couldn't remember. He had been too stoned. The family, somewhat quelled by the thrashing, left threatening police action if Buttermilk did not rein in her son.

Distraught, Buttermilk went to the local political leader. This was still the Communist era. The elderly man advised Buttermilk to marry Bonomali off. Everyone around her added further weight to this suggestion. Buttermilk knew she couldn't stay home to fix her son; she began to believe that a wife might settle him. A girl was found: Bhokti, fourteen, low caste and pretty as an angel. Bonomali was seventeen at the time. The marriage was illegal, the bride being under eighteen and the groom under twenty-one. That was the least of Buttermilk's worries since the law is rarely enforced. Her focus was on a course-correction for Bonomali; if marriage didn't do it, fatherhood surely would. Bhokti was a means to that end, not a full-fledged person with a separate need for well-being.

The couple's first night together had apparently passed without activity. Buttermilk had deployed a young neighbour to tease out reports from Bhokti: neither man nor wife seemed interested in sex. Bhokti, a slip of a girl, blithely skipped about the courtyard during the day, and slept soundly with her new husband at night. This had gone on for several weeks when Buttermilk decided to intervene. She recruited Rikta, who was already married by then. Her husband Sumit took Bonomali aside and tutored him on the business of birds and bees, while Rikta tackled Bhokti. The training worked, and within four months Bhokti was pregnant. This was a landmark victory for Buttermilk, on two counts. First, it redeemed her son's innocence on the charge of sexual assault. 'If he had truly done that,' she argued, 'wouldn't he have pounced on his wedded wife? He didn't even know the game and had to be taught!' Second, to her great relief, it proved her son's virility. She would use this a decade later when Rupa's parents, upset over their daughter's childlessness, pinned the blame on Bonomali.

At fifteen, Bhokti was mother to a baby girl. But contrary to Buttermilk's hopes, fatherhood left no mark on Bonomali. He carried on being a full-time loser. When his baby was about six months old, he outdid himself. Penniless and frenzied for his next hit, he stole from a couple who lived next door. He was in a drugged haze and got caught in the act. Buttermilk was away at work when this happened. As she neared her home that day, she noticed that a large crowd had gathered around the lamppost next to her gate. She lunged, her heartbeat quickening, and burrowed through the throng. Bonomali was lashed to the lamppost, blood streaming down his face and injuries all over his body. He was limp by now but several men continued to pummel him. 'Stop,' Buttermilk wailed, 'if he's done something, take him to the police! Stop hitting him!' She cradled Bonomali's lolling head: 'What did you do, babu? Want some water?' The mother's angst turned the crowd off; it dispersed. Besides, the punishment had already been meted. As she untied her son and scraped him indoors, there was more in store. Triggered by Bonomali's theft and his public flogging, Bhokti had swilled some urea believing that it would kill her. Buttermilk found her petrified on the bed, the stench of thrown-up urea all over her, waiting for death. She recovered soon enough, but the light in her eyes had gone out.

About a month after this, Bhokti poured kerosene on her herself, struck a match, and threatened to set herself alight. Bonomali was the only other person at home that day. As he wrapped himself around her to stop her, she let out a terrifying scream. When the neighbours came running, she testified that Bonomali had tried to burn her to death. This was a very serious charge. Physical abuse of brides is so rampant in India that it is the alleged perpetrator on whom the law places the burden of proof. As a serial substance abuser with a chequered past, Bonomali would've been on thin ice. In the event, the police didn't press charges since Bhokti had no visible injuries. Her parents had arrived. Distraught at her state but more worried about a future with a divorced daughter, they tried to counsel her into staying in the marriage. But with help from the local women's commission Bhokti made up her mind: she was going to leave with her child. She was not yet sixteen.

The next morning Bhokti's parents gathered up her belongings: two saris and a few odds and ends. Buttermilk, resigned to the outcome, returned the gold ring that Bhokti's father had given Bonomali for the wedding. As Bhokti left with her parents, her child in her arms, the neighbourhood gathered for the spectacle. A bride was quitting her marital home after a hair-raising event. There was gruesome theatre in this, like a road accident.

*As they walked to the station, I went along for a bit. I took the baby from Bhokti's arms for a last kiss and cuddle. My heart was breaking into a million pieces. We were passing a Brahmin home, and the woman of the house came out on the porch to say goodbye. So we stopped. That's when I did what I did. You see, when the baby was born I had made a silver bracelet for her and slid it onto her plump little wrist. It had tiny silver beads that would jingle as she moved. I took that bracelet off. I took it publicly.*

*I said, 'You're my flesh and blood. The day you come back to me, I'll wrap you in silver from head to toe.' Look at me, I'm getting goosebumps talking about this.*

*Anyway, seeing me do this, the Brahmin woman said, 'What you just did was not right, Aunty.'*

*Those words, and her disapproving glance! That Brahmin's curse is what has destroyed my life—my son's future, my husband's health, my land—all of it. I've been paying for it ever since. Taking back that bracelet. That sin, it's a nail stuck in my heart.*

In a fresh tragedy, the child died a year later. She toddled, unattended, into a pond. That incident, more than his wife's departure, definitively broke Bonomali. But Bhokti survived. Four years after the break-up—three after losing her child—she remarried. In early 2016, Buttermilk heard that Bhokti had just given birth to a daughter. 'My youngest sister Chutki is in touch with Bhokti,' Buttermilk said, explaining her news source. 'When she was pregnant she'd told Chutki: "I'm really craving something sour now. For my first time, my other Ma had made oiled mangoes for me. I wish I could have some of that! My husband has brought home a pile of green mangoes. Aunty, can you teach me the recipe?" When I heard this, believe me, I felt someone had lit a furnace in my chest. If she came and stood near me once, I'd feed her oiled mangoes to my heart's content. Seeing her new baby's face would perhaps take the sting off my heart.'

Buttermilk chalks up her troubles to divine retribution that is well deserved. Searching for atonement is how she rises above her losses.


The day I sat down to write about Bhokti walking out with her child, Buttermilk skipped work unannounced. I knew she was fighting fires on several fronts and that her explanation later would make perfect sense. But this didn't help. A dust storm the evening before had left my flat bathed in grit. I felt it under my feet and on my desk. In a Kafkaesque distortion, it enveloped the grit in Buttermilk's life that I was trying to write about. The sharp edges of my power over her became stark. I should dock her wages, I found myself thinking, on a bilious impulse. The absurdity in this quickly reared up and reined me in. But had it not, she would've had absolutely no recourse.

When pitted against those she serves, no one stands with Buttermilk. In the eyes of the Indian state, she is not a worker; labour laws don't apply to her. The reasons have to do with constrained definitions of a 'workman', 'workplace' and 'employer'. In an extension of dismissive attitudes towards unpaid housework, what Buttermilk does for pay does not qualify her as a workman. Applying labour laws to her workplace raises concerns of the state's overreach into private households. And confounding the usual mapping of a single employer per full-time worker, piece-work maids, who weave their own housework with paid shifts, have multiple employers—Buttermilk has six. Her work therefore remains unprotected by India's Workmen's Compensation Act 1923, Trade Union Act 1926, Payment of Wages Act 1936, Minimum Wages Act 1948, Maternity Benefits Act 1961, Equal Remuneration Act 1976, Inter-state Migrant Workers Act 1979 and a host of others. Unlike factory workers, street vendors, or cab drivers, maids like Buttermilk have no unions. An estimated 10 million domestic workers, overwhelmingly female, have essentially no access to grievance redressal or collective bargaining.

A community of activists have been strenuously trying to change this for the past thirty years. Since a Domestic Workers Bill introduced in 1989 fizzled, there have been repeated attempts at passing a comprehensive national legislation to recognise, regulate and protect domestic work. Bills have been introduced in 2008, 2010, 2016 and 2017. None have seen passage. In 2010 the Indian government directed its states to extend their minimum wage legislation to domestic workers. Wage laws vary from state to state, and most states have not complied with this central directive. There have been minor breakthroughs, however. The Unorganised Workers' Social Security Act 2008 recognised domestics as wage workers for the first time. The Sexual Harassment of Women at Workplace (Prevention, Prohibition and Redressal) Act 2013 included domestics in its ambit, thereby obliquely recognising the home as a workplace. But neither law addresses the issue of domestic workers' rights.

Why has such a law proven so elusive? Perhaps because entrenched cultural norms sap this issue of political will. A law truly looking out for the welfare of domestic workers would tug at every urban pocket, middle class and up. Even those engaged in the cause of domestic workers—activists, trade union leaders, bureaucrats, politicians—all employ maids at home, and a steep wage hike might give them pause. Further, there is the pervasive fear that empowering domestic workers would rupture well-tended class membranes. In 2000, West Bengal's Department of Labour refused to register a union of domestic workers to avoid being flooded with employer–employee disputes and the ensuing complications. At a meeting in 2013, the Union Cabinet expressed concern that allowing domestic workers to unionise would lead to law-and-order problems. Well-paid and empowered domestic workers would be contrary to the interests of India's vast urban middle class whose political clout is significant and growing.

In September 2012, a task force employed by the government submitted to the Labour Ministry a Draft National Policy on Domestic Workers, recommending a modest minimum wage of 9,000 rupees per month for full-time domestic work, in addition to maternity leave and fifteen days paid leave annually. A National Policy is merely a guideline, not a legally binding statute. Even so, the one on domestic workers was still pending in April 2018. Meanwhile, in June 2011, the International Labour Organisation adopted Convention 189, on Decent Work for Domestic Workers, which codifies the rights, protections and systems of justice to be accorded to domestic workers worldwide. India has refused to ratify it, stating that its national laws were not yet in line with the provisions of the convention. Even if such laws were to be enacted, in a culture of enforcement that is at best weak, it would be a necessary but hardly sufficient step. The outlook for real change in the rights landscape of India's domestic workers is therefore grim.

Ancient India had done better, at least in terms of laws—we know little about enforcement. India has had servants in one form or another for over two millennia. The earliest Indian text referring to the rights of domestic workers is the *Arthashastra*, from the third century BCE. Chiefly a text on statecraft, it covers a wide range of topics, from military strategy to economic policy to law. Within book three of the *Arthashastra*, titled 'Concerning Law', chapter thirteen is devoted to laws regarding dasas—variously, slaves or servants. There is much in this chapter to at once thrill and depress workers' rights activists, including a rather progressive law against sexual assault and rape of female domestics. Modern India does not have such a dedicated law; in passing the Sexual Harassment at Workplace Act 2013, maids were folded in as an afterthought and enforcement is rare. But the most compelling law in chapter thirteen is one that ensures wage payment of servants by creatively leveraging the Indian psyche. 'Neighbours shall know the nature of the agreement between a master and his servant,' the law reads, thereby offering protection to the servant through a threat of social shaming of the master. Over 2,300 years later, Buttermilk does not enjoy this protection.

Those fighting for the rights of India's domestic workers are nearly all women from the urban elite. The maids themselves, poor and often illiterate, are strapped with gruelling schedules and have little free time. In the absence of unions to fall back upon, skipping work to show solidarity quickly becomes unaffordable. Worse, in many cases, the maids remain unaware of the hard-fought benefits their elite sisters-in-arms have wrought for them. In abstract matters—rights, for instance—even awareness costs time. But this disconnect runs apace for more pedestrian benefits as well.

For about a decade starting 2001, an NGO in Calcutta maintained a resting shelter for commuter maids like Buttermilk. A room had been set aside at Dhakuria station to enable the women to freshen up, rest and relax between shifts. The hope was that the shared camaraderie would be empowering for the women. Dhakuria station, adjacent to the Ponchanontola slum, was on Buttermilk's daily route. But in all those years, she never found out about this shelter.

17

# In the Reach

'Some of these women are huge, like elephants!' Buttermilk said, her arms open wide. 'Most are Marwari, some Bengali. Their joint pains get worse in the cold. That's why they need me.' She was talking about her massage clients. Winter was back in the city, bringing woollens and foul air. For Buttermilk, it brought longer workdays. In the winter months, she takes on massage shifts on top of her usual jobs. The work is hard but nearly doubles her income.

'Then there are the others,' she went on, 'who want skin titment.' Treatment, to improve the tone of wintry skin. 'They get me to massage them with kirim.' Cream. 'They go fully naked, only with panties on. And they say: 'O Aunty, harder, harder, yes, that's better!' My fingers feel like they'll crack. My own joints ache. One knee has gotten creaky.'

'So you need massage too,' I interjected.

'Sure, I get a massage every night,' she shot back. 'Don't you know?'

'Really, who massages you?'

'Why, god, of course!' She broke into a guffaw. 'If god didn't massage me every night, how am I getting up each morning and running around?' Then on a sober note: 'It gets dark by 5 p.m. now. By the time I drag myself home, it's 7 p.m. and feels like midnight. Dark when I leave, dark when I get back. I feel like a wrung towel. But the money is good.'

With the added workload, she needed to eat lunch on the go. 'I get really hungry but I can't digest street food. And who's going to pack lunch for me at 5 a.m. when I leave? The only thing I can eat is mishti.' Bengali sweets made of milk curds. 'But even that is not without trouble. The other day, while walking towards a massage home, I felt like I would pass out if I didn't eat something first. I saw a mishti shop, went in, and said: Dada, give me two mishtis. So the man gives me two, pretty big ones. I hand him a hundred-rupee note. You know what he gave me back as change? Forty rupees! I thought: thakur, that expensive? But I had to ask: how much are they? He said: why, thirty each. My ears were ringing. I had already bought them, couldn't give them back. That'd hurt my pride. I left the shop and walked away while eating them. Then I felt: what is this that I'm eating? My mouth, my heart, my body—all getting soothed, like my Ma's caress! The mishtis were entirely nolen gur, with liquid centres. Aaah, I've never had anything so wonderful! But even as I felt this, I thought: look at you, eating pricey mishtis alone. Have you ever fed such mishtis to your children? Or your parents? Pretty soon I began to cry, even while swallowing those lovely morsels.' She had marked the shop as one to be avoided. 'Every time I walk by it, I burn up with guilt. Imagine, I ate sixty rupees worth of mishtis alone! Such a dripping tongue! Chee chee chee!'

In late February, Buttermilk brought me turmeric corms, fresh off her village harvest. 'Here,' she said, 'keep as many as you want.' I had wanted to eat slivers of raw turmeric, a seasonal pick-me-up. As she handed me the corms, I noticed her bright crimson nail polish.

'You should eat some too, you know,' I said, 'it's good for you.'

'I don't have time to eat poison,' she deadpanned, 'and you're giving me turmeric!'

I laughed. 'You have time for nail polish, though!'

'Thakur has said,' she said, smiling, a sweet light playing in her eyes, 'work hard, fight battles, do whatever, but never deny yourself what you fancy. Mine is this: a dot on my forehead, vermillion on my parting, and nail polish on my fingers and toes. Only red, mind you, nothing but! My daughters keep me supplied, and I have to remind them: make sure it's red!'

I could see that Buttermilk had nice nails, their beds long and deep. She kept them trimmed but her work had still chipped the polish off the tips. I thought of her wisdom in picking a fancy that was so easily fulfilled. But there was more to the red than that: it was a reflection of her marital status. All red would be drained from her life as a widow. Buttermilk had cannily wrapped Jhoro's life into her fancy.


At fifty-five, Buttermilk had now begun to take stock and ponder old age. Her books were a tango of pluses and minuses. She had worked every day since she was six. While she didn't get ahead, Buttermilk had certainly beaten the odds: she hadn't fallen through the cracks. She had forged a life in the city without giving up her life on the land. Her landownership was on uneven footing, but her city home was rock solid, both in paperwork and function. Jhoro was in indifferent health, unable to work, but at least not chronically ill. She was highly valued everywhere she worked but would've liked to prune down her gruelling schedule. She couldn't, as Bonomali had to quit his factory job and now made only half as much as a day-labourer. As an upshot, he had been in a relatively steady state since. Buttermilk's dearest wish now was for a grandchild from her son. 'My home is blind without that,' she said. 'No one to light the bloodline.'

On balance, they—Buttermilk, Jhoro, Rupa, Bonomali— seemed to be on a rest-of-the-life groove in their Subhashgram home. Buttermilk didn't believe she could ever really retire. But she actively mulled over the future, weighing moves, as if on a chessboard. Much of this was spurred by her worry for Bonomali.

'I've decided to give one of the Subhashgram rooms to Mamata,' she said. 'I'll do it in writing. This is for after my husband and I are gone.'

'Why would you do that?' I asked. I thought Mamata was well settled in her marital home.

'She lives in the village. When her girl is older, she'll have to think about her future, her schooling. What if they need to come to the city? She'll need a place.'

'Makes sense,' I said. Rikta didn't need this support since she lived in the city.

'Aah, but that's only part of it,' Buttermilk said with a calculating grin. 'What I really want is for Bonomali to have a sister living with him when I'm gone.' Helping Mamata was the side effect. Her main purpose was to ward off a possible take-over of the house and eviction of her witless son.

Buttermilk didn't trust her son to ever take custody of his own life, much less her home. But in a future without her, the question of land loomed the largest. On a recent visit to the village, Dhobo, one of Bonomali's cousins, had pressed Buttermilk to bequeath her land to him. 'Like vultures,' Buttermilk fumed, 'I'm not dead yet and they're already wheeling! But can I blame them? They see Bonomali does nothing on the land. And getting Rupa to even visit is like pulling teeth!' In response to this, she had hatched a ploy. 'I told Bonomali and Rupa: "Look, you two won't go to the village. Dhobo lives there and is asking for the land. I'm thinking I should give it to him." They immediately yelped: "Innhh, where would we go except to the village?"' Buttermilk was pleased with their response but had little confidence that it would convert to action. She saw unskilled jobs drying up in the city, machines taking over much of the labouring work, the only work her son was good for. She worried that Bonomali might fail to feed himself someday, unless he worked the land. 'So I told them: start visiting the village every Sunday. I'm not asking you to go during plantings and harvest. But say there's a crop on the land, just go in and weed the fields. In between crops, plant veggies. Go and tend to them. Plant flowers. Let folks see that you care about your land. That you mean to stay. Otherwise, when I'm gone, you won't be able to keep it, I'm telling you!' With threats and tutorials, Buttermilk tries to instil the land in her son.

She tries, but she's not very hopeful. 'I couldn't make my son stand,' she said one day with a sigh. 'I'm thinking of old age now. My body is breaking, I can tell. You know, I've carried so much stuff back from the city, from construction sites, to build my house. A ton of rubble, bit by bit. At least 2,000 bricks, three or four at a time. The other day, I saw a pile of stone chips and was sorely tempted. Remember the new toilet that the government has given us? When they did that work, they dug up my yard. A layer of stone chips would do it good. But I got scared. My knee gives me trouble nowadays. With a heavy load of stone chips, what if I fell? I've gotten old!' she said with a disbelieving smile. 'I don't know how many more years I can work like this.'

She had ideas for an alternative. 'My veggie patch, next to the coconut palm—I'll ask all of you for advances and build a room there. I'll rent that out and keep working a bit. Between the two, I think I'll have enough.' Then she switched channels and turned on a locavore's dream.

'Whatever happens will happen. I'll work as long as I can, then go live in the village. No shortage of food there. Rice is a given. I could easily sow lentils in the winter: yellow peas, grass peas, mung. No end of veggies. Then, say, I could keep a few chickens. That'll give me eggs and meat. I could raise fish in my pond, or even my ditch. So what's left?'

'Oil,' I ventured.

'I could do that too. I've done mustard before. Crack it to get oil. I could do sesame as well. That oil is even better.'

'Salt, then?' I wasn't giving up.

'Yes, I may have to buy salt,' she conceded, laughing. 'But you know, even that we learned how to do when we were kids. It's the Sunderbans, you see, our grandmothers knew about salty earth and where to scoop it out! You dissolve the earth in water and hang it up in a terracotta vessel. The water seeps and gathers in a pot below, which you then dry out to get salt,' she finished, with a child's glee.

But this was a reverie, she knew. 'The land won't feed me if I don't feed it first,' she said. 'The question is: which feed is easier.'

'I sometimes wonder,' Buttermilk said, 'what did I really do with my life?' A celebrated singer had just died in a horrific car crash and there was marathon coverage on TV. Watching this had brought on thoughts of her own legacy. 'I saw his body there in a glass box, a flood of people streaming by, giving him flowers. Look, I'm getting goosebumps. A tubby boy placed his bouquet and dissolved in tears. He'd come running from college. How far was his college? He was sobbing so hard he couldn't speak. And I'm thinking what this man must've done to leave so many in such a state! And what have I done? When I die, will even a fox or a ferret move a muscle?' She had tried to turn this into a teaching moment for her son. 'I told him: look at this, if you make your mark, this is how people show their love and respect.'

Buttermilk lives this lesson herself, largely through giving. She can't afford to give as much material help as she would like. But she gives freely from her formidable arsenal of life hacks forged over time.

'My husband's uncle's son came to me recently: Aunty, find me a job, I want to move to Calcutta.' The rural youth was newly married and the sole heir to a vast tract of land. But disenchanted with his farming trajectory, he aspired to a life in the city. His educated—and pretty—wife clashed daily with his mother. 'So he's bought her a dog!' Buttermilk's eyes flared at the absurdity. 'Dogs are more expensive than humans. Besides, in the village, there are all sorts of contact taboos. The dog keeps touching them and they all have to go bathe again! It's a circus!' The pet clearly didn't solve the youth's problem. He wanted to get away from his parents. He would work for a living in the city, and when his father passed he would still get the inheritance.

'I told him: you want to work. Do you know what a job is? I do laundry and floors—that's a job. The man pushing a pen at an office—that's a job too. I truly believe work is work. But he's thinking: I'll go to the city, do something shiny. Many years ago, I used to see this man on the train each morning. Spiffy clothes, shoes shined. I was sure he worked at some fancy office. One day, I'm taking a shortcut through the Lakes and I see him. Guess what he's doing in his spiffy clothes: he's walking a dozen dogs! I told this boy: can you be a dog-walker, for 10,000 rupees a month? He groused: I'll start a business. Okay, what's a business? Go to Baruipur, buy a basket of guavas, take a train to the city, squat at any station and start selling. They shove you out from one spot, you move to another. If your profit at the end of the day is 300 rupees, that's a lot. Or, you're farming rice here—take rice to the city and sell it at profit. Or take vegetables. That's how you start. Take a cycle-van on the train, pay the luggage fare once—100 rupees. Then arrange to park it somewhere in the city, that's 100 rupees a month. Now you have wheels. Bring your fare—fruits, vegetables, whatever you're selling—to the city by the morning train, and hawk it all day long in that cycle-van. Roam the city, figure out the cracks, the footholds. That's how you work and build a life. Doesn't happen overnight.'

As Buttermilk disabused the youth of any notion of shortcuts, his parents sat next to him, in tears. 'It was gratitude!' she said, incredulous. 'They thought I was discouraging him, their only child, from leaving them. But I really was trying to teach him to start out in the city.'

'I want to share what little I have,' she explained. 'The Marwari family I work for owns a cow. They get their butter churned from fresh milk'—she rolled an invisible vertical pin between her palms—'and don't care about the gallons of buttermilk. The servants divide it up. Some sell their share. I give most of mine to neighbourhood kids in Subhashgram. Let them have some too! Whenever they see me, they cry: there she is, Aunt Buttermilk!' she smiled. It is not her real name, but one she enjoys.

Of late, Buttermilk had been dreaming of travel. Nothing drastic, just her first vacation. On a pilgrimage, naturally. Only inscrutable city folks go to the beach or the mountains with no pilgrimage attached. One sparkling morning in spring, she said: 'Listen, I might go away for a month.'

A month? 'Ah, don't worry,' she brushed off my alarm. 'I'll make special arrangements for you. To the others, I won't say a peep. I'll just disappear. Its only twenty-seven days, not a full month.' I was thrilled to be special in her book. But where was she going?

'To the mountains,' she said, breaking into a luminous smile, 'on a pilgrimage!'

'Really? That's fabulous! Which mountain?' Her excitement was contagious.

'I'm not good with names, Himiloy or Himloy? It's a big group. Sleeping, cooking, eating, all in the bus. They're asking a lot. But I've kept them hanging. When there are empty seats close to departure, they'll have to drop the price. Good strategy, no?'

This was the 'Kundu special' model of Bengali travel, tailored for the underclass. I was swept up in visions of her sampling India's sublime pilgrim geography. Was she going alone? She was suddenly shy. 'No, no, I'll have to take my man along. You know, we've been married thirty-six years and we've never gone anywhere together. When I went to Rajasthan with the Marwari family, I went alone.'

And then on a thoughtful note: 'I'm wondering, will this really work? It's a lot of money. And I have debts galore. If I take on new debt to go on pilgrimage before settling the old, how will I show my face to the gods?'

She dangled this vision of a mountain pilgrimage for weeks after this. It brought a spring to her step, vigour in her work. It eventually faded but would periodically come back. She seemed to have figured out how to marshal the nourishment in going away without actually doing it. While in this mode, one day she asked: 'What's an ocean?' She had never been. I tried to describe breakers, how they crash and spray you with spume, how the sand gives way as the wave recedes, tickling your feet. She giggled with delight.

'Is the sand like what's dumped at construction sites?'

'It can be. Or it can be white like powdered sugar, or even black. Sometimes there's no sand at all, but smooth pebbles.' It felt wrong to ratchet up the longing in her eyes. 'Why don't you take a couple days off and go to Puri? It's close by and cheap. You get the ocean as a bonus with the temple.'

'I've heard so much about Puri. I really want to go. Just not finding the time.'

It wasn't until several months later that a trip materialised for her. Not to the mountains for twenty-seven days but to the sea just for a night. Technically, not even the sea. She was going to attend a fair at Gangasagar, where the Hooghly opens its maw at the Bay of Bengal.

The day before leaving, she recited her itinerary yet again, her thrill boiling over: 'Don't forget, I'm coming in early tomorrow. We'll catch the 2 p.m. train from Subhashgram. It's a huge group! Us four, Rikta–Mamata, their husbands and kids, and four more!

On the train until Namkhana, then we catch the ferry. We have a place to stay at an ashram. But I'll roam the fairground all night!' Her eyes shone, like bright plums. 'My first vacation ever and I'll spend the night asleep? Won't happen! At first light I'll take a dip at the confluence. Then the fatigue will hit, so I'll take a nap. Leave in the late afternoon, back home by night. And back to work the next day!' She was taking exactly one day off.

She returned alloyed by travel. 'I took a dip as the sun rose and the moon set. The tide was in. Huge waves, chest-high! We stood facing them holding hands and jumped together as each rolled in. Such fun!' She giggled. 'I wanted to hold my husband's hand. But he was too scared of the water, my poor broken man!' The ferry ride, especially, stayed with her. They had boarded just before sunset. 'I saw that huge orange ball melt into the water,' she said, 'and the water turned vermillion, with gold flecks. Hundreds of birds—swirling in the air, landing in the water, catching fish. And all around, endless water. Maybe one or two sandbars now and then. No trees anywhere. All that emptiness and us a dot in it. I've never felt this way before.'


'Did you see how the sky had dressed up earlier?' Buttermilk asked. It was an overcast morning, threatening to rain. 'I saw it out the train window when coming in today. As the sun rose through the clouds, the colours leached out all around, just like a printed sari! I was glued, couldn't get enough!' I had missed it, like most dawns in my life. But I saw it now, struck by her imagery, both vivid and uniquely hers. Printed cotton saris, cheap and central to Buttermilk's life, have bold colour blooms that often spill the lines meant to contain them. I saw her watching the scene from a moving train, packed to the rafters with maids commuting into the city.

'Oh, oh, here come the fat drops,' she cried on her way out. 'I'm off!'


Buttermilk's path has always been a sharp ridge—a precipice is never far. An injury that doesn't kill but maims her, draining both work and resources. A serious illness for Jhoro. Bonomali walking into yet another crevasse. A flare-up on her land. Any of these could happen, any day. Regardless, Buttermilk will rise at 4 a.m., catch the 5.40 a.m. into the city, work her six homes, and her massage gigs if it's winter, get home, eat dinner, watch a bit of TV and go to bed. Those potential futures stalk her, she knows. But on the train to work, she will watch the radial rays of the new sun skewer grey clouds, making their edges bleed.

18

# Epilogue

On bad days, Buttermilk blames Karno for her Atlas life. Then she remembers him in that in-between year, between the assault and his death. No one had the faintest hint that Karno was considering suicide. No facts emerged later that he may have been running from that year—no debts or other liabilities. Except perhaps a slow insight into Mejo's animus. 'Maybe Baba had begun to believe that he deserved it,' Buttermilk presents her best guess. The attack had left Karno deflated that year; he was not his large and full-blooded self. But he was working. He was drinking with his buddies. And towards his children he was more loving than ever. 'A quieter and sweeter Baba,' Buttermilk remembers.

*That year he also helped me out on the land. I had decided to go ahead and do the amon crop even though both my husband and I were working in the city. If you let land lie fallow in the rains, all sorts of vultures turn up. So I had to turn to Baba for help. And*

*Baba did the lion's share. He used to bicycle from his village to mine every day. An hour's ride each way. His head swathed in a gamcha to hide the shameful scars from the assault. You know what I regret? Since I don't like taking time off without good reasons, I never went to see Baba during that entire season he worked my land. He would arrive at daybreak, work all day in the field, and go back home. He never once stepped into my in-law's house. He didn't want anyone to notice his stitches and get curious. After the paddy came up, he took charge of spraying the pesticide. He even helped out at the harvest. That was late November. And by early January he was gone.*

*One day that year, he bought ocean crabs from the Raydighi market. He came home and told Ma, 'If only Mejo-ma would come today'—he called each of us girls 'ma' and and the boys 'baba'— 'these crabs are such beauties!' Then he recounted the story of me catching that large crab nearly thirty years before. Ma set a couple of crabs aside and cooked the rest saying, 'I'll call her. She'll come.' I didn't know any of this, of course, but for some reason I felt a tug to go see them that very day. I caught an evening train after work. As I walked in, Baba was on the porch. Seeing me, he leapt onto the courtyard and broke into a hilarious jig, like a string puppet!*

*He looked thrilled and kept saying, 'Thakur heard me! He's brought her over!'*

*I was taken aback, I couldn't tell what was going on. Baba kept dancing.*

*I asked Ma, 'What's the matter? Why is he dancing?'*

*Ma grinned and said, 'I'll tell you. Come, sit. Have some dinner.'*

*'I just ate before coming, Ma,' I said. 'I don't need dinner.'*

*Ma said, 'You've eaten, fine, but you'll eat some more now. Then I'll tell you what's going on.'*

As Ma served up the food, I was flabbergasted! There was catfish braised with radish and on top of that, crab curry.

I said, 'Babbah, this is a real feast! You got crab today!'

At this Baba came over and said, 'Now you know why I was dancing! I bought the crab and couldn't stop thinking of you. And the time you caught that crab when you were little. I really wanted you to come eat with me today.'

Tears were streaming down his face. Ma was crying too. We all carried that foiled feast within us. This time though, I ate the crab with rice. Baba sat next to me as I ate, watching my every mouthful.

As I left the next morning, Baba stuffed two live crabs into my bag, their claws rubber-banded—the ones Ma had set aside. Then he came to see me off, carrying my bag all the way to the bus stop. The bus pulled away, he waved and called out: 'Enjoy the crabs, Mejo-ma!' He had a big smile, his eyes sparkled. That's the face I think of when I think of Baba.

Karno Haldar had righted one wrong.

# Acknowledgements

I am that odd Bengali who wrote not a word in youth. Writing came to me mid-age, thanks to the faith and encouragement of Purnendu Mitra and Nayantara Patel. Ajitha G.S., editor and security blanket, has been the best custodian this book could have hoped for. Suneetha Elluri and Prof. Jayati Ghosh have generously shared their scholarship on domestic workers.

Thank you, Ma, for unabashedly championing every piece I've ever written. And thanks always to Steve Capell, my runway for all take-offs and landings.

The one I wish to thank the most has insisted on anonymity. It is to her that the book is dedicated.

www.ingramcontent.com/pod-product-compliance
Lightning Source LLC
LaVergne TN
LVHW011010200726
843509LV00011B/1040